Charlie Ross was born in Glasgow ...
and the Isle of Skye. After studying at the University of
Edinburgh, he spent eight years as a teacher of Physical
Education and then lecturer in sports science.

In 2000 he embarked on a career in stand-up comedy which has
proved to be successful, performing at many of the top
comedy venues in the United Kingdom, including the world
famous Comedy Store in London.

His comedy career has led to several acting and writing credits,
with one film script in pre-production at the moment and
several other projects in the pipeline.

SMILES AND TRIBULATIONS

CHARLIE ROSS

To Stu
An inspirational and
friend
Thank you!

Charli Ross
x
2013

Smiles and Tribulations
By Charlie Ross

First Published in the UK in September 2010 by 100 Publishing
An imprint of Hirst Publishing

Hirst Publishing, Suite 285 Andover House, George Yard, Andover,
Hants, SP10 1PB

ISBN 978-0-9566417-4-8

A CIP catalogue record for this book is available from the British Library.

Cover Design by Robert Hammond

Printed and bound by Good News Digital Books

Paper stock used is natural, recyclable and made from wood grown in
sustainable forests. The manufacturing processes conform to environmental
regulations.

www.hirstbooks.com

"Angels can fly, because they take themselves lightly"

- *Stephen Fry*

PROLOGUE

About a year ago, I had just come off stage at The Stand comedy club in Glasgow. It was a packed Saturday night, 200 plus in the room. The gig had been a belter. Really. An absolute cracker. As you will find if you read on, and hopefully you will, I am my own worst critic - so you can take me at my word when I say, I blew the roof off the place.

I went to the bar for a self-congratulatory bottle of beer. While waiting for my drink, one of the audience, a smaller man in his thirties came up to me. He shook my hand, looked me in the eye and said, "That was brilliant, mate." I thanked him as one should, and then he said something to me that led me here. "So, do you know any real comedians, then?"
At that moment, it occurred to me that in this X-Factor, uber-celebrity world, anyone in this business isn't taken remotely seriously unless they're "that guy off the telly".

Other comments that come your way are,
"So, do you get paid for that?"
"You got a real job then?"
It doesn't occur to many of them that there are many comedians, possibly hundreds, who are working away week in, week out, earning a steady (maybe sometimes not-so-steady) income. It's a job! And this is the story of one of them.

Who do I thank? Well, all my friends who supported me in the early days, and didn't say, "COMEDY? Don't be so daft, ya long streak of piss!"

Gus Beadie, Huw Griffiths, Mark Izatt, Gordon (Starky), Sue Aitken, Alex Heatherington, Iain Houston, my sis Katherine and nephew wee Ross – well, he was wee then! Many, MANY of my students.

7

Latterly, Paul Dillon, Harry Emambocus, Davie Macahill for his "sound" sound help, Calum, Stewart and Jim - how much camera time do I owe you? And loads more.

I especially need to thank the following friends and wonderful comedians for their contributions to this book. They have been entertaining and invaluable.

Fred Macaulay
Stu-Who?
Scott Agnew
Viv Gee
Des Mclean
Sandy Nelson
Ian Cognito
Janey Godley

Laugh of my life

Nobody can begin to imagine the exhilaration, the rush, the sheer energy of feeling the laughter of an audience: storming at you like a tidal wave onto the stage. For Roxy Music, love was the drug. For a stand-up comedian it's the laughter. It is all consuming, addictive and you never tire of it. As long as they are laughing, the world is good. Well, at least for the time you're on the stage. It's a high; intoxicating and sexual all at the same time. But as with every high, the lows of a stage "death" can be hard to recover from. That is, of course, if you're self aware enough to notice, many "comedians" aren't.

For delusion is also a big part of the game. As is illusion. To an extent, it's a magic act, a trick, maybe even a con. And like any piece of magic, if the audience can't see how it works, if it can't see the joins, then the comedian has won.

Amongst all the performance mediums, stand up is unique. It doesn't adhere to the "fourth wall" required in theatre performance. In fact, it is necessary to blast that invisible wall away, and the best comedians do that with gusto. It is also alone in that the demands to come up with fresh new material are enormous, particularly for those lucky enough to make it big and get that all important TV show or DVD release. It's great, but once it's out there, the gag/joke/ routine is gone, forever. Madonna can go on singing "Like a Virgin" until the day she dies, the Royal Shakespeare Company will continue to hash out Hamlet regularly, and the producers of the Bond films will, well, go on making Bond films. And yes: there are always new stunts for 007 to perform, new songs for Madonna to sing and new ways of staging the Shakespeare greats. But the essence is the same and always will be; you can keep getting away with it. Not so for the comedian. If the great Billy Connolly did a

"Greatest Hits" tour, even he would probably be very harshly criticised. The style can be the same, the tone and rhythm of your voice can be a constant, but the material has to be new, fresh and most of all, funny.

This is not going to be a "Ten Steps to Being a Comedian" book, or a bitter rant on the "How come he made it and I didn't" scenario. Just one moderately successful comedian's attempt to have a look at the ins and outs, the ups and downs, and the stormers and the deaths in the life of a stand-up comedian. Although I can't promise that bitterness won't be there... Without a spot of that, most comedians would get nowhere.

As I write this, I have just entered the "Scottish Comedian of the Year" competition, an event that is just four years old. This is the first time I have entered. Why? More of that later when I discuss comedy competitions in general, but I shall be inserting diary entries as I progress. If indeed I do progress, these diary entries may be a very small part of this work - certainly from a personal point of view - but I shall endeavour to follow the competition from a personal and general viewpoint.

Getting Started

Today, stand-up comedy is the new rock 'n' roll. Comedians are playing the kinds of arenas usually reserved for Robbie Williams. Stand-up comedians are all over the television, be it on the Paramount Comedy channel, or Michael McIntyre's Comedy Roadshow. Comedy clubs all over the country are packed to capacity. Even in times of recession, comedy still thrives, maybe especially so. People want to be cheered up, they want a different night out, and an evening of comedy can do the trick. All comedians start somewhere, though. Everyone from the top of the tree like Frankie Boyle to comedians much like, well, myself, all came into comedy at some point. Usually as a squirming, sweating, nervous wreck in that very first gig. It all starts somewhere. There is a saying among alcoholics – that it's not the last drink which gets you drunk, it's the first. The first gig can pretty much have a similar effect.

I can sum up my beginnings in stand-up comedy in one word. Procrastination. I talked about it, mulled it over, played around with ideas, threatened to do it for a very long time. Maybe two years. What a wasted two years they were. The material and ideas I have gathered in that time were not very different from the five minutes I eventually performed. At the time I met a guy I vaguely knew, we drank in the same pubs – again, more of that later – and after chatting I found out he was a stand-up comedian. I knew he was an actor but had no idea that he had performed stand-up too. After a brief chat one evening, I confessed to him my ambitions, and thankfully he was very encouraging. It would, of course, be rude of me not to tell you that his name is Neil Shackleton, and amazingly, ten years after that conversation, I have yet to see him perform. But he did give me one fantastic piece of advice, and I am now going to pass it onto you. This quite simply has served me well for many years and I am indebted to Neil for it. It was this:

"Don't perform material that you *think* the audience will find funny, perform what *you* find funny."

This may be an obvious point to make, but it is amazing how many people I see trying stand-up, struggling because they are trying to pander. It's easy: unless you genuinely find what you're doing funny, unless it has made you laugh out loud when you wrote it or thought of it... Toss it. Because if it ain't funny to you, then how the hell is an audience going to find it funny?

And so the road was now marked. But here's a thing. I had never, ever, been to a comedy club. I had seen many comics live over the years and countless more on video and DVD, and as I've said in the prologue, listened to them on vinyl. But a standard comedy club with the usual compere plus three-act structure? No. And this was to lead to my first failing. And boy, was it a big one.

Along I went to what was then the best-loved club night in Glasgow - The State Bar - with its inimitable host, Billy Bonkers. To say Billy was ok at stand up, no that's not fair. He could get a crowd onside, and had some nice stuff. I think he himself probably knew he was never going to light the touch paper of the comedy world. But he knew comedy, he knew it when he saw it, and he put together one of the best clubs I've ever played. Like all good comedy clubs, the State Bar should never have worked. For a start, it was tiny. A minuscule basement bar, with a stage that barely had room for the amp speaker that blasted the vocal to the audience, often way too loud for the size of the room. Plus, and I kid you not here, lit by a bedside lamp. Honest to God. But the audiences were packing the place, when it was busy it was hot, sticky, uncomfortable, (then) very smoky, and you could never get served in the short breaks that allowed you to. But boy did it have atmosphere. At times it was electric, and when he got it right, a good skilled comic could have them eating out of his hands. At the time there was a club running in Paisley (I never got to play it, as it sadly closed before I had the chance to get my name down) and Billy Bonkers was always clever enough to book their headline act to open the State Bar. Hence the club would very often have a cracking line-up. That night featured the wonderful Mitch Benn (very funny, and a fellow Doctor Who fan to boot), and the enigmatic brilliance of Stu-Who? (a Scots act who has been around since the dark ages, and looks it, but is among the best at his game).

It was fantastic. I fell in love with comedy that night. It was then I realised that I had only dabbled with comedy before. This was where it really happened. I can remember the energy pulsing through me as the laughter rattled around this tiny basement. I loved it, and I was hooked at that moment, never to look back. So, at the break, waiting for Stu-Who? (his full stage name includes the question mark) to close the show, and with my heart jumping in my chest, I took those first brave steps up to Billy Bonkers and asked him the question that would change my life for, well, the last ten years I suppose! I asked him for an open spot.

At this stage I should explain what an open spot is. If you know what it is then you may want to skip this paragraph. But it is the first time that a comedian performs in front of an audience. It is usually placed at the top of the second part of a comedy show and usually lasts about five minutes. At the time, five minutes seemed like an eternity. How the hell was I gonna fill five whole minutes? I knew I could talk for five minutes. Up until then I was a full-time teacher of Physical Education, and at that time I had been a lecturer in further education. So I knew that talking for anything up to an hour was well within my grasp. In fact I could, on occasion, get some laughs out of my students with odd quips and one-liners to settle them down before the serious stuff. But this was five minutes that had to contain constant and sustained laughter. Could I do this? Billy took me totally by surprise by simply asking if I wanted to do a bit that night. I declined quicker than Muhammed Ali could land a punch. But the next Thursday – game on.

I rushed home and looked at my material. Formed it, tweaked it, ordered it. And, remembering Neil's advice, was confident that it made me laugh. But what about other people? I asked two mates, Gordon and Alex, to come up to my flat and listen to it. What happened is to this day, one of the worst experiences I have ever had. You see, folk often say to me, "How can you stand there in front of hundreds of people and talk?" Well hundreds of people are easy. Believe me. There is, first of all, more chance that a larger portion will find you funny, and a large crowd creates a wave of euphoria of its own. They build a unity and a trust and any notion of being self-conscious at your own laughter is gone. Ten people? Six? Or on this occasion, two? That's torture.

So there we were. Gordon on a chair, Alex on the couch. And me, standing in front of the telly. Ready to go. And I did it, the entire five minutes verbalised and given life for the very first time. How did it go? Lots of big smiles and Alex occasionally quipping, "Oh yes, that's very funny!"

As I said, torture.

But they did actually like it, and I trusted them enough to tell me that I was kidding myself on, it's crap, you can't do it, take up macramé.

Not everyone takes their first steps into the world of comedy in the same way. At that time, an evening class in stand-up comedy was being run at Strathclyde University. There are plenty of such classes running now – I run one of my own now and will come to that in a separate chapter – but a Scottish comedian called Viv Gee ran this one and it has to be said, it was ahead of its time. The year I took my first steps into comedy was a strange one, and as it turns out, an important one.

The 90's in the Scottish comedy circuit were quiet. What is now referred to as the "alternative scene" was in its infancy, and was very low key in Glasgow. Ed Byrne, the hugely successful Irish comedian, studied in Glasgow and started a club at a bar called Bachus. The State Bar was running, as was Blackfriars.

But then comedy wasn't the huge queue of hopefuls lining up to be stand-ups that it is now, so there wasn't a great deal of comedians to support regular clubs, without bringing acts up from England, which is expensive. That's not to say there weren't some exceptional acts at the time in Scotland. Stu-Who?, Bruce Morton, Fred Macaulay and Phil Kay to name a few had enjoyed considerable success making TV and radio appearances, as well as Arnold Brown who won the Perrier, and Rhona Cameron. The late 90's saw the emergence of Janey Godley, Paul Sneddon, Frankie Boyle, Joe Heenan and Raymond Mearns, all of whom would go on to be a source of support to me, and were fast establishing themselves as hard-working and reliable acts and in the case of Frankie Boyle, comedy superstardom. The Stand comedy club in Edinburgh was growing and would emerge as THE main club in Scotland, later opening a hugely successful venue in Glasgow.

When I started in 2000, a strange thing occurred that is yet to be repeated. To stay in stand-up for ten years is a fair achievement. A lot are gone within six months to a year, most give it up within three. To maintain any degree of success is to walk a difficult path marked with hard work, scene politics and public relations. Not everyone is cut out for that, and if I've had the "That's it, I've had it, I give up" late night phone call with one of my friends once over the past ten years, I've probably had it ten times. It's tough. So if the odds of just making a living in this game are short, then the odds of getting real success are minuscule.

In one six month period during the pivotal year of 2000, the following acts embarked on their comedy careers.

Des Clarke
Scott Agnew
Des Mclean
Rev Obadiah Steppenwolf (Jim Ure)

All of those acts have gone on to have considerable and successful careers, the main point being, that ten years on, they are all still working in comedy. Whether you have seen any of these guys perform and, if you have, whether you have liked them or not, they have stayed. They have done enough in this game to carve some kind of career in the business. And that is in itself an achievement.

For Deses Clarke and Mclean, the journey started at the very class ran by Viv Gee at Strathclyde University.

Competitions

I've always thought competitions in the creative arts were something of a misnomer. There are no set criteria. All they serve to do is set the mood of the time. When "Chariots of Fire" won the Best Picture Academy award in 1981, it led to a spate of worthy period dramas that ultimately gave the film world Merchant Ivory. But was it the best film? Of course not: few, nowadays, have seen it and it has been buried so deeply in movie history that it serves only to provide the occasional bit of nostalgia and maybe be used as a reference point for teachers of A level Physical Education (I know what I'm talking about there). I'm not saying it's bad, it's actually pretty good. But it ain't the Godfather, or E.T., or Raging Bull. Films which many still talk about with great verve. So what did the award mean? Simply put, it established careers. Those involved were guaranteed a fruitful career, or at least the opportunity to create one. They were in the shop window. They had been noticed.

Comedy competitions provide the same service to the lucky winner. Like many other competitions in the arts, they set the tone, or reflect the zeitgeist. But do they go to the funniest comedian? Invariably not. They do tend to go to funny comedians, but funniest? Again I emphatically say, no. And how can I be so sure? Because nobody knows who the funniest comedian is. There is no way of measuring. There is no tool that says one person was 15% funnier than another. And what do you do, count the laughs? That would just be ridiculous. Comedy competitions invariably view the entrant over about a 5 – (maybe) 10 minute set, but anything over 7 is rare. Billy Connolly sometimes does one set-up in 5 minutes. Many comedians do. So there we have another condition. It is often the competition for the comedian who best performs in a small set. Rather to the exclusion of those who take their time, or whose laugh to minute ratio is smaller.

Like all such competitions, it's a subjective decision, made by those "in the know". Promoters, TV producers, and other comedians. Selected because, as we all know, promoters and TV producers are never wrong when it comes to identifying talent. They know it all. Once again, more of that later.

The comedians tend to fall into a few categories. The "new talent" competitions that were very trendy when I first started but have less credibility now. The BBC did one, Channel 4 also sponsored one. Aimed at those who were reasonably new to the world of stand-up. Criteria ranging from time since first gig, or amount of paid work the artist had received. A series of national heats would result in a high profile final, usually at the Edinburgh Fringe, and some guy from London with an agent would usually win. Bitterness? Yes. Truthful? Frequently.

Actually, competitions are one area in which I have very little bitterness, because in truth, I'm dreadful at them. Or at least the people who ran them and judged them thought as much. So I never really paid them much heed.

Do they have a purpose? Yes. To the performer it can be exposure to influential promoters, agents, television and radio commissioners. Are they an accurate barometer? Not often. When Jimmy Carr (one of the most lauded, successful and revered stand-up comedians of our time) entered the BBC competition, he only got to the semi-final. Is the winner that year now more successful than Jimmy Carr? Well, his name is Jason John Whitehead.

Yes, that's the pause I was expecting. Now Whitehead is a very good comedian who has a very successful career. And maybe I'm misjudging him. Maybe he was offered a television career with loads of money and stardom and didn't want to go down that road. Believe it or not, even in our celebrity obsessed culture where everyone allegedly craves fame more than anything, there are some who don't want all that. The point being, that there are many competitions that have thrown up that very scenario. But the judges know best.

In fact, a lot of the entrants to these contests invariably are clearly more experienced than they give on, making the criteria and therefore the very nature of the event, pretty redundant.

The other competition takes a very different form. I shall be spending some time on the Edinburgh Fringe Festival in a chapter devoted to it, such is its significance to many stand-up comics. It's hard to do this job and not be drawn into its clutches. I shall be paying it closer scrutiny then.

Every year, there is an award at the Edinburgh Fringe for the best comedy show. Another for the best newcomer. And another for the most innovative.

Many know this award as the "Perrier". And for many, many years, the established suppliers of (as it turned out, politically dubious) bottled water sponsored this main competition. Judged by a team of "experts" who go to see all shows that are eligible. If they like it, to be fair – and I like this – they go see it again, to be sure. Now don't get me wrong. The process by which the winner is chosen is generally fundamentally fair. Shows are scrutinised and seen by different people. And then whittled down to a shortlist and, eventually, a decision made.

I wish to use an Oscar analogy again. Recently, actor F. Murray Abraham was asked how the Best Actor Oscar for Amadeus changed his career. He simply said that he had never been out of work. Now Abraham is a fine actor, an excellent one. He didn't go on to forge out the same kind of career as a Tom Cruise or a Brad Pitt – neither of whom possess an Oscar. - but he has always worked.

Demetri Martin
Will Adamsdale
Laura Solon
Phil Nichol
David O'Doherty

Now the winners of the "Award formerly known as the Perrier" similarly may not be household names. The above list is a selection of past winners. But I'm sure they haven't had many weekends off since winning. They have probably been able to guarantee a career from the success. But what of the major DVD releases, appearances on TV panel shows media attention? They are all post-millennium.

The 90's were a rather different story.

Frank Skinner
Steve Coogan
Lee Evans
Dylan Moran
The League of Gentlemen
Al Murray

In the year Skinner won, the runners-up were Jack Dee, Eddie Izzard and Lily Savage.

What has happened? Has stand-up gotten worse? Has the quality subsided? I don't think so. I just don't think those who make the big decisions are paying that much attention to competitions anymore. Even the event itself has struggled to find a sponsor. At the time of writing, the Fringe is well underway, and no sponsor is in place.

Has the competition died? I think it's certainly in critical condition. The dominant newcomer awards have no TV coverage anymore. And when even the main gong at the world's biggest comedy festival is dragging itself around, there is certainly an argument that the whole notion of comedy awards is dwindling. They will always be around. But the currency is dropping. Share prices are low.

One reason could be that the judges stifled what comedians were doing. They set a trend that said they were looking for a "show," with a theme, a structure. Not just the run-of-the-mill stand–up but evidence that the performer can put a narrative together. Well, I'm afraid that's not stand-up. And that is reflected every year in the myriad of "why didn't he just do his usual stand-up stuff" type reviews that appear with growing frequency. In 2003 I tried just that in a show called "Tracksuits and Munchkins." The show was to analyse my love of the film The Wizard of Oz and also my addiction to football. Basically looking at my contradictions, a man who lives in two worlds. That of the masculine, ladsy PE teacher and the camp old world of gay scenes and disco music. And it was fine, got good reviews, audiences enjoyed it. But boy, was I bored by week three. And it showed.

To me, and again like everything this is a personal thing, there is an element of the jazz riff to comedy. The great comedians always gave the impression that they could go off on a flight of fancy exploring the comedic possibilities of a moment. Improvising off a comment from the audience or the reaction to a previous routine. Or just coming up with routines off the cuff. There is freedom. Not restricted by the lines of a play, or the set of a rock band, but free to wander. In this world of "the narrative," I felt constrained. Restricted. Claustrophobic. This is not stand-up to me. This is a one man show that happens to be funny. If there is too much structure, if the beats are programmed and you can set your watch to the timing of the gags, then it's not stand up. In an effort to give the judges what they want, many comedians have done just this. Maybe removing that room to breathe is why the Skinners, Izzards, Brands, Evans and Coogans aren't coming through the Fringe anymore. I doubt very much that any of those guys would follow the restrictions of a theme or narrative. They do what all great comedians do. Just go out there and make people laugh.

That's it.

And yet here I am, in 2009, putting myself back into the competition mire. Madness? Maybe. The main reason was predominantly to do with this book, to get myself onto the grassroots level and see what's happening in Scottish comedy.

The Scottish Comedian of the Year was inaugurated in 2006. Unlike a lot of other competitions it is open to absolutely anyone who was either born in Scotland or has lived here for some time. If he wanted to, Billy Connolly would be free to take part. In fact I wouldn't be surprised if he did one year, just to do a famous television show about it. That's another good reason to enter this year. Thus far, he hasn't been tempted.

11ᵗʰ August 2009

Entered the Scottish Comedian of the Year competition today. Took me a long time to decide. This is the fourth and, to be honest, I always thought it was a poisoned chalice, kind of a lose/lose scenario, unless of course you win. But what the hell, if I get to the final and do well, then at least I'll be able to challenge the judges to put aside conventional thinking and see if they have the balls to give it to a poof two years in a row (fellow homo Scott Agnew won in 2008). So either way, and again the big caveat exists that I have to perform out of my skin - if I lose, I can drudge out the old "they were never going to go for the gay guy again" line, so maybe this is the best year to enter.

As I am writing this, a new competition has emerged. In June 2010, Take The Mic, sponsored by The Sun newspaper, boasts the biggest prize money in comedy competitions - £1,000 for winning a heat, and £12,000 to the overall winner – and is open to any Scottish or Scottish based comedian. With heats in five cities: Aberdeen, Dundee, Inverness, Glasgow, and Edinburgh.

Entry was through the website, where competitors were invited to place a clip of their work on You Tube. These would be scrutinised and whittled down to seven or so acts for each heat. The outcome was fairly interesting. Now, I did enter, but being very lazy, left it too late, had a rubbish clip on You Tube and wasn't even available for the heat I got into. C'est la vie!

The set up for this competition is quite interesting. In the heats, each comedian will perform an eight minute set, judged by a panel of experts combined with an audience vote. The final should be very interesting; the lucky heat winners will get to play five nights at the Edinburgh Fringe and will be judged over the run, instead of on a one-off. How is this better? Well, anyone can have a one-off good night or bad night. A totally inexperienced comic could pull one out of the hat in a final whereas a better, more talented one could, in theory, have a stinker. Over five nights, it's also more likely that consistency will emerge.

Anyway, the heat that everyone SHOULD have climbed over themselves to get into was the Inverness one. A mediocre selection of open spots and relatively new comedians, but the line up did include the current "Scottish Comedian of the Year." Interestingly, and here is the bizarre nature of competitions in the arts, he didn't win. Instead a pretty inexperienced open spot triumphed on the night, taking the grand, and getting into the final.

The Aberdeen heat was won comfortably by a local act - sorry that sounds unfair - the act in question, Gus Tawse, is a very strong comedian. But a home advantage can only be a help, not a hindrance.

The Glasgow heat was a curious one. Many good acts, myself included, avoided it, thinking it would be highly competitive. As it turned out, the standard was pretty much like the Inverness one. With, again, a relative newcomer - albeit a very talented and bright star for the future - Mikey Adams, emerging as the victor.

The Edinburgh heat, conversely, was the one to avoid. Heavily over-subscribed and with a higher standard, which included, curiously, an act called Greg McHugh who has found some degree of success in a TV show called "Gary Tank Commander." I always thought the idea behind doing competitions was to give you exposure to GET ONTO the telly, not to do it after the event. It runs the risk of backfiring.

Will your TV exposure and support of an agent and PR be enough to carry you through? As it happens, no. It did backfire. The heat was won by something of a Scottish comedy veteran in the excellent John Scott. Ach, I'm sure Greg's ego will survive.

The Dundee heat was the last gasp, and this throws up, for me, a controversial area of stand-up. The line up had some excellent comedians, including my best friend in comedy and extremely funny Scott Agnew, another former Scottish Comedian of the Year. The heat was in fact won by a sketch double act called How Do I Get Up There. Now, before I go any further, I want to emphasise that these guys are good, very good. I wouldn't be the least bit surprised if they ended up on TV very soon. And Chris and James who form the act, are nice guys, real diamonds, and in fact very good stand-ups in their own right. However, sketch comedy is not to my mind, stand-up. So here's why I think this.

First, the rules are different. The key to making something stand-up, as I've mentioned elsewhere, is the complete non-existence of what is termed "the fourth wall", the invisible wall that exists in a play for example. The audience can look through this wall, but the actors must build this wall in their minds and create a closed off space. Now, do actors sometimes pierce through that wall? Of course they do – frequently in fact. That does NOT make them stand-ups. A sketch show is scripted, it exists within the confines of four walls, therefore that dynamic is different. Second, by its nature, the audience's reaction is different. For a start, at the end of every sketch they are almost definitely guaranteed an applause. A reward usually reserved, in stand-up, for an exceptional routine or gag. Even the best don't get that on every gag. A stand-up will oftentimes gauge the success of his set on the number of applauses he gets. When it's more or less guaranteed, is that the same thing? It's like bankers getting a guaranteed bonus, well it's not a fucking bonus then! So the audience view the performance in a totally different way. Thirdly, by its nature there is no interaction with the audience other than dramatic delays for laughter. In a sense, sketches are mini-plays. But the ultimate argument surely, is this: if there were a SKETCH competition, would I be allowed to enter and do stand-up? You bet your boots I wouldn't! Now it's not Chris and James' fault. They entered, and were invited to perform. But I reckon for next year there has to be a re-evaluation of that aspect of the entrance rules. The ultimate irony being that a heat for a competition called "TAKE THE MIC" was won by an act that never once used a mic!

Obviously I have discussed this with other comedians; some have agreed and some very much disagreed. My argument is simple - if this competition was for a comedy PERFORMANCE, then frankly, the bloody Python team could enter. But it was a STAND-UP PERFORMANCE. And I think that's different, it's what makes the stand-up different.

Who knows what may transpire from this? Suffice it to say, that I'm pretty confident that competitions will always be around. Would I advise other comics to enter? Of course, for one reason and one only. It's stage time. And that's what all aspiring and experienced comedians need. It's another gig, and if there is even a modicum of talent there, then every time you perform, you get that little bit better.

August 20th 2009

Saw the list of the other SCOTY entrants today. No-one that makes me feel particularly threatened, but then I'm going into this with an open mind. Well, at least I'm telling myself that. I'm trying to convince myself that I'm going in as a curiosity, an observation, even an experiment. Truth is, the more I think about it, the more I want to win it. Can't believe how stupid I was to think that my ridiculously competitive nature wouldn't creep into this. So I not only want to be the best on the night, I now want everyone else to die on their arses. I'm a worry to myself sometimes.

25

Stage Time

From the first minute of the first open spot that any aspiring comedian performs, they are on the road to being better, funnier, more polished. It is the learning curve, the qualification, the rite of passage. Only stage time can offer this. Of course, feedback, analysis and a large helping of self-awareness are absolutely imperative. But stage time makes the comedian. And it leads to one very telling question.

How much stage time is needed before you can call yourself a comedian?

The point at which someone can rightly say to someone, "What do I do? I'm a stand up comedian, mate," is a hotly debated one.

Woody Allen's character says in "Broadway Danny Rose" that it's one hundred gigs. Now I'm not usually one to disagree with Woody Allen. The man's a comic genius and knows what he's talking about, having cut his teeth in comedy clubs all over the States in the 60's. But I know plenty of people who have done over a hundred gigs and I still wouldn't call a comedian. Conversely, I've witnessed comics who would have been entitled to use the term comedian after thirty gigs, and they are better comedians than I will ever be.

So is there any quality control over stage time? Again, that is debatable. Some will advise that access to any stage is useful. And I would agree, tough rooms can be just as valuable as easier ones, even if it just means you articulate your material, get a chance to think on your feet. And, well, a tough room is just that, tough for the time you're up there but with little effect on either your career or personality. That is another key to stand-up.

I will go on to talk about good gigs, bad gigs, competitions and their pitfalls, the Edinburgh Fringe, free gigs, charity gigs; but the bottom line is, the one thing they all offer is stage time. There does come a point in a career where it is prudent to be selective about the gigs that you accept - however, in the early days, grab every opportunity you can get. Even bad ones. If only because it will demonstrate to the new comedian whether he/she can handle it or not.

Sunday 23rd August 2009
Got my date for first round of the SCOTY today. It's on 5th September at Uisge Beatha, a comedy night in Glasgow's West End. In fact, I'm doing The Stand that night and the heat is after that, so I've got a great warm up. The others in the heat are mostly newish apart from Viv Gee, pretty much a veteran of Scottish live comedy and Rab Brown, a finalist from last year but only in his second year at the whole thing. So, being honest, I fancy my chances. Top three go through, so in all honesty if I don't there will be a very humble entry next week. Am I nervous? Little bit. It's only 8 minutes and I need to pick my stuff carefully. See how it goes.

Don't take it personally

A lot of our material is personal. We have invested time and effort into it. And then ultimately stood on a stage and bared our souls. If the audience don't laugh, or heckle you, it's very difficult not to be wounded. But you must learn to make the hurt short-lived and move on. Anything less will result in a very short comedy career, although ultimately tough rooms can be counter-productive and should be played less and less as the career progresses. Especially if you're doing ok in other gigs. If they're all tough, well, it's macramé again.

Having said that, it is the personal material that I like the best in comedians. I enjoy someone who shares experiences, although often exaggerated for comic effect, and I think that is something of the special nature of stand-up comedy. It is as I've mentioned elsewhere, a conversation where only one person is doing the talking (in fact, that is pretty much like any conversation with a stand-up comedian, our egos often don't allow for anyone else to get a word in). I often find that the more personal the material, the more the audience engages with you. They appreciate you sharing, and often, especially in an extended show, you can be sharing some very personal stuff. I have spoken on stage of my parents dying of cancer, of failed love affairs, of moments of despair. And I am also proud that I made the points I wanted to make but still in a comic context. Although discussing the death of my parents was a challenge, but when you go through something like that, it is very much humour that gets you through, both during and after the experience. In fact, it is probably that turbulent and emotional experience that drove me to doing something like stand-up comedy. It is only after such tragedy, when the fragility of life comes roaring into your life like a steam train, that you realise very quickly that *all* the clichés are true. Life *is* too short. One really *should* grab opportunities. But again, it doesn't matter how personal you make your material, it still has to be one thing, yes, you know what I'm saying!

Now of course, those who just tell jokes and gags, and make observations are just fine as well, it's a personal preference, I was brought up on Billy Connolly talking about his experiences on the Govan shipyards, on Richard Pryor talking about failed marriages. But I also have a deep love for the surreal magnificence of Woody Allen's stand-up: he tells us NOTHING of his personal life through this medium, but yet would go on to study his own relationships and emotions through his movies.

Plus the advantage to that form of material is that the audience share the experience. Talking about family, sex, school, relationships makes it easier to connect with the audience as they have, for the most part, experienced those things. That's not to say that you can't talk about climbing Mount Everest, just because the audience probably won't have done that and therefore won't connect with you. But the connection with familiar territory certainly helps.

Saturday 5th September
First round tonight. Got a gig at The Stand (Glasgow) first, so that should be a good warm up for the SCOTY. Never know with these things. It's an audience vote so they may go for you or not, plus I'm sure some other entrants will bring mates. I suppose if that's the case I just have to aim to be everyone's 2nd favourite comedian of the night. Surely that would take me through!

Clubs

They come in all shapes and sizes, they do. There are a number of expressions that pop up in comedian chat all the time.

"It's a weird shape, that room."

"You know, the gig just shouldn't work there, but strangely, it does."

I was once booked to do two gigs in two nights in Kent. One in Maidstone, the other in Rochester. It was a strange booking, there was only one act, and each night was for £200, so not bad money. I turned up in Maidstone to this pub. It was a fairly ordinary boozer. Not overly busy, a pool table raised up on a mezzanine, and the rest pretty standard. I went over to the barman and told him what I was there for. He confidently replied, "Yeah, you're over there mate, I'll get your microphone, start in 20 minutes?"

He pointed at the pool table and walked away. I was worried. He reappeared a few moments later with a mic and stand, and plonked them in front of the pool table telling the two guys playing that this was their last game.

They did NOT look happy. Neither would I have been, actually, I like a game of pool.

At that moment I did something I have never done before or since. I had a drink. I think that particular pint of lager went down in record time.

The countdown had ended, the time had come. I gingerly went up to the microphone in front of the now deserted pool table. For all the love in the world, I was about to tell them to keep the money and ask over the microphone if anybody wanted a bloody game of pool.

I tapped the head of the mic gently, the gentle tap resounding throughout the bar. There was one table of about eight people right in front of me. And the other twelve odd people were randomly scattered throughout the bar. At this moment you just have one thought in your head.

GO FOR IT!

If they like you, fine, if not then at least you gave it a bash. It is highly unlikely that anyone of any influence in the comedy or entertainment industry is going to be there, so what the hell.

I began. I talked about how bewildering it must be to have this arbitrary Scotsman standing up, interrupting their chat, disturbing their drink and generally making a nuisance of himself. To my amazement, they listened. A minute later they were laughing. After ten minutes I had them. Now there was one mitigating factor. My previous occupation as a teacher was a bonus. The table of eight in front of me were all teachers having a night out. So I lucked out, to a degree. The gig was fantastic. And it shouldn't have been. One guy, for over half an hour, with no stage, no light and only a misused pool table for back-up. I should have left there with my tail between my legs. I was very pleased, and a little proud.

By the next night, my pleasure and pride had regenerated into confidence and a little smugness. The drive to Rochester wasn't without concern. I have concern and anxiety about every gig. I welcome it. But I thought, it couldn't be as bad as last night - and if it panned out even half as good, then that would be a result.

I walked into a busy, quaint and traditional English pub. It had a buzz about the place. A definite atmosphere. In the corner of this L-shaped bar (never a good design for entertainment) was a small stage, a backdrop, microphone and stand, and a lovely soft spot of light washing the stage. Hey, this looks good. This place has been set up. Now, whenever you're booked for two or three gigs at a time, you always factor in that one of them will be tough, even a nightmare. So clearly last night's was the nightmare that I had got away with. I had dodged the bullet. I couldn't wait to take to the stage. What happened over the next forty or so minutes will stay with me forever. I still wake up in the middle of the night in the coldest of sweats.

To say that the gig was a nightmare is like saying that open heart surgery is just a graze. Nobody listened, and those who did sat with faces so blank, Van Gogh would have started painting on them. At the end of the 34 minutes, it felt like 34 hours. "The English Patient" felt like an episode of Terry and June in comparison, and I left the stage. I walked sheepishly over to the manager of the bar and firstly apologised. I then said I would only take half the fee to cover expenses.

His response amazed me.

"Don't worry about it mate, everyone dies here. Stu-Who? has been down here three times and he's dying to crack it."
That, I was not expecting. And this happens. Gigs create personalities. And the weird thing is, that is whether they have a regular audience or not. Reputations grow, and an audience can act accordingly.

This is not to say that the fault can't lie with me, the comedian. Although I performed the same set, same routine, same smile... the difference between performing well and not well is tiny. Musicians often say that the best gigs they play are when they're hungover, tired and edgy. Then they go for it because they are aware of their frailties. You dig deep. Maybe the second night I had already performed the gig in my head, the previous night having lulled me into a false sense of *yadda yadda*, you know what I mean. But the gig can be a bug-eyed monster that is coming to get you.
There was a club in Glasgow, in a bar called Blackfriars. It ran every Sunday, was compèred and run by a lovely and very funny comedian called Viv Gee. When I started in 2000, it was

one of the city's most prominent nights for comedy, and everyone played there. It had one of those reputations.

"Blackfriars is difficult."

"If you do well at Blackfriars, then you're doing well."

Comments like that.

Weird thing is, the club itself didn't particularly draw a regular crowd of people. Maybe on average, you would get the same faces in two or three times a year. But when they walked through the door, paid their money and sat down, collectively as a group, they adopted a persona. They had learnt, been told over a period of time that they were a difficult crowd. And they behaved accordingly. Conversely, the gig that everyone in Glasgow – Scotland - dare I say the whole of the UK - wants to play, is The Stand (Glasgow) at a weekend.

To say The Stand is a great gig is again an understatement. When I'm booked in there, it is highlighted with a marker in my diary as one that I can't wait to do. The room is great, the audience better. Most comedians up and down the country will tell you that they can't wait to do it. Now don't get me wrong. You can't get away with murder. They wont laugh at just anything. They are however, forgiving and polite to acts who aren't doing that well, and if you're close to funny, then they will you to do well. If you don't, the attitude generally is, "Well done for trying, thanks for attempting to make us laugh."

You're probably thinking that the demographic must be very different to that of Blackfriars. Amazingly, no. In the same way as one group of people in Kent decided to love my act one night, and a very similar group of people collectively loathed me the next, the type of people who go to The Stand are very similar to those who went to Blackfriars. The club has a personality. And audiences react accordingly.

Now, luckily, as your career develops you may have the luxury of being able to decide which gigs you do or don't do. Avoiding the tricky ones and focussing on the nice ones. And comedians themselves have a very different take on this. Some focus on the good ones and avoid the gigs that will be harder work. What is the root of this?

Some could say it's playing it safe. Some could say if you need neither the money nor the challenge then, why bother. Stu-Who? clearly loves the challenge. Because quite frankly, if I hadn't eaten in a month, I still wouldn't play Rochester again.

The Late Show at the Edinburgh Fringe has this reputation. Now this has a very singular demographic. They're all pissed. They want to be entertained but, and this is the most dangerous audience of all, they want to be noticed. A drunk audience, or even audience-member, has the unfortunate desire to build their part up. A need to offer more to the proceedings than just laughter and applause. The Late Show is, as many call it, a bear pit. Only the fittest and the strongest survive. Me? I don't particularly want to do that. I will if asked and paid, but Ben Elton said in the early days of the Comedy Store that the show was mostly crowd control and that's where he developed his aggressive style. To me, that's not allowing the comedian the breathing space needed to be funny, to get the well-formed and thought-out material out there, to get the respect that all performers in other fields get. Listen first, judge later. The comedian in a difficult club is judged as he goes. It's like a big Gong Show, and it only allows a certain kind of style – quick-fire, gag-oriented... whatever you want to call it – to succeed. Bear pits, hard gigs are limited. Good gigs are open to all possibilities. And that is what a successful comedy club is all about.

Sunday 6ᵗʰ September

Well, I got through. As I thought, one act had a crowd in and the winner also had a load of mates in, putting me third. Was I better? Well, I had a great gig, and the reaction seemed to be better than anyone else's, but that's fine. Job done. Semi-final next Sunday. Although, I'm starting to work out that in order to progress in this kind of set-up all you have to do is be everyone's second favourite. That way you sweep with enough votes, so theoretically, you could win this and still not be the best in anyone's books!

Promoters

Remember this. A comedy club promoter is free to book whoever he or she wants. It's not a public service. Most comedy clubs, and definitely all the big ones, are a business.

They exist to make someone money. Simple as.

So when a promoter doesn't book you, it is easy to storm off in a huff. It's easy to take it personally. That is not to say that some of the decisions made by promoters in terms of setting up a gig may be a little odd, strange or sometimes downright bewildering. And yes, sometimes I do not doubt that it is personal. They just don't like you.

Those of course are often the bad business people.

Good acts can get booked.

Good acts can NOT get booked.

Bad acts should not get booked but sometimes do.

Sometimes, a bad act will get booked when a good act is overlooked.

If that happens, then the promoter doesn't know what he's doing. To not book someone because you don't think they're right for your club, that the style and material isn't your cup of tea, is fine. To not book them because they don't like you is ridiculous. And not good for business.

So who are promoters? They are many and varied.

1. Business people who have seen an opportunity or gap in the market. They may have a venue to utilise and think that a comedy club will be perfect for a spare night.

2. Someone who likes comedy, not a performer but someone who has a passion for it, knows about it and wants to put on a show. These guys are often in rural areas and want to bring something different to the locals.

3. Ex-performers who aren't very good and want to get stage time.

4. New performers who want to get stage time, and get to know other acts and the ways of the business.

Bottom line, promoters tend to hold all the cards. Without them, the comedian makes no money, without the comedians, they make no money. It is a two way street, and that's something that promoters should occasionally remind themselves of. The problem with numbers 3 and 4 of the above that there is the possibility that these guys will be mates, fellow performers. There is an old adage that friendship and business (particularly money) don't mix. And of course you get on better with some of these guys than others. Favouritism can cause problems, even resentments, and it's not as if comedians need an excuse to bitch about other comedians. They just do, for the same reason a dog licks its balls. Because it can.

Nothing Compères to You

As I've pointed out, a comedy club night has usually four (maybe five) constituent parts. An opener, a middle spot possibly preceded by an open spot, and a headliner. The glue that binds all that together is the compère.

The role of the compère is vital and anyone who thinks it's an easy task or that if you can do a solid twenty minute set you will automatically be able to compère, then you are sadly mistaken.

The role of the compère is vital and, tragically, can be thankless.

Sandy Nelson, who aside from playing William Wallace's older brother in Braveheart (among many fine acting credits), is also one of the UK's best musical comedy acts and compères.

"Some people say to me after compèring a gig, 'that was great mate, you should try real comedy.'"

And usually they're not kidding. Compères can be the forgotten or lost souls of a comedy night, yet their role is vital. To use a sporting analogy (and I know a lot of people hate those but it's what I know), they say in football that you know a referee has had a brilliant game when you haven't noticed him. A compère, for me, is a little bit like that.

The compère sets up the night, getting the audience in the mood, explaining the ground rules – don't heckle, switch off your phones, give the acts some respect – in fact compères will often invite the audience to heckle them instead of the acts. So basically, by its very nature, compèring compels you to set the acts up as the most important element of the evening. Bad compèring involves ego, when a compère sees the night as an opportunity to showcase him/herself, and basically just does their own material in the stead of talking to the audience and getting a reaction from them. Basically, taking the heat out of them. An audience has a potential to be like a boiling pot of water, a good compère should bring them to the boil then put them on a simmer. I know what is it to be a bad compère because I don't really feel I am a good one, certainly not compared to the best in the game.

Raymond Mearns
Mickey Hutton
Scott Agnew
Susan Morrison
Joe Heenan

These are guys where if you see them on a bill as compère, then you know you're in good hands.

Sandy says there are skills to remember, and these don't always involve skills onstage. There are backstage skills before you go on.

"Know the acts' names, ask if they have any needs or specific introductions, or even information to avoid. I worked with a Canadian act recently whose first joke is about the audience thinking he's American, so if I introduce him as 'all the way from Canada' then his first line is screwed."

Onstage then, your job is to warm up the audience, to get them tuned into what's going on. Oftentimes, an awful lot of the audience will never have been to a comedy club. They won't have a clue what's going on, and may only have ever seen Micheal McIntyre's Comedy Roadshow, or Live at the Apollo. They are big theatre gigs, event gigs if you will, with names that we are generally familiar with. This is all very different from a live gig. It's smaller, more intimate, and there is a responsibility for the audience to grasp it that one doesn't have when watching the TV. The compère should do all of that, but in a funny way and in about ten minutes.

Try, where possible, to use as little actual material as possible. This is your chance to allow the audience to vent any issues they may have wound up inside them. Get it out of the way, then the acts can focus on doing the material they have prepared. That's not to say that an act won't, or can't, take advantage of that. If the compère finds out that someone is a teacher, then I, as an ex-teacher who talks about that in my routine, will almost certainly use that. Sandy goes on,

"You don't necessarily have to react to things immediately, the advantage of compèring is that you are going back on stage again, so you can come back to something, and you may even come up with a better line."

Be aware of the kind of act coming on. The way you introduce them is vital. If they are a quiet act then you don't want the audience going mental as they come onto the stage. Conversely, if the act is loud and brash then you should work the audience up for the energy level appropriate to who's coming on.

I have nothing but admiration for compères. At their best they do a fantastic job, and can make you as the act feel comfortable knowing that the audience is well-prepped and ready for you. It gives you a tremendous sense of comfort when preparing to do your act. And thanks to all of those great compères who have helped myself and others have good gigs over the years.

Sunday 13th September
I said this part of the book might be a short one, and there you go. I'M OOT! Beaten again by people who brought mates that helped the voting, and although I was fourth and apparently it was very close, that doesn't matter. I'm gone. But that's ok. I could very easily have brought a load of mates in to vote for me, but as one of the more experienced acts on the night, that would not have reflected too well on me. The Scottish comedy world is a small one, and it would have got around very quickly that Charlie Ross only progressed cos he brought a rent-a-mob! I'd rather go out with my head held high. Weird thing is, I feel no shame, no indignity and well, I don't really care. The final is often a good gig, and that was sort of what I was looking forward to. Ho hum.

I Never Read Reviews

Lots of people in this business say that. In fact, so many say it that it leads me to believe it's bullshit. Of course they do. Well I do, all my mates do, and especially at the Edinburgh Fringe you have to. A good review is an essential marketing tool at the Fringe.

Reviews in comedy tend to work on a star rating ranging from poor one star to excellent five star. This system, which is currency at the Fringe, has pretty much been adopted to review comedy in most other mediums as well.

I've had a few, and they have for the most part been quite favourable. Over three Fringe shows, I've never had a review lower than three stars, which is certainly pass marks, and have had a couple five stars. That does feel good.

The main advantage to a review is, as I've said, marketing, pure and simple. Of course there can also be a clever use of wording. Reviewers are now becoming very careful not to put a phrase or wording that could be misused or interpreted in a manner opposing to the intent.

For example, and this is a crude one but here goes.

"Charlie Ross managed to display a brilliant range of ineptitude, misfired gags and over indulgent nonsense" - *The Daily Paper*

Now that would be a bad review, and can I emphasise, it is NOT REAL! But there would be nothing to stop me printing a poster that said,

"...brilliant...."
- The Daily Paper

That kind of thing goes on quite a lot, and there is really nothing to stop anyone doing it. So reviewers have cottoned on, and a bad review usually leaves no wiggle room.

I remember in one Fringe show there was a comedian in the same venue who shall remain nameless for no reason other than to name him would just be unfair. He is a successful and hard working comic, and got a severe two-star review. It was published in a paper called "Three Weeks" which is only printed for the duration of the Fringe. It's a useful guide to what's hot and what's not, but also not really a publication that is considered the pick of the crop. A good review is welcome, but what you really want is one from the national press, or the respected comedy websites such as chortle.co.uk.

This comedian panicked and fired round the venue picking up all the copies of "Three Weeks" minimising the amount of people who would see it. A slight overreaction, but the weight of any review in the Fringe is so intense that it makes you a little nutty about things, and a touch obsessive.

Do acts occasionally make up reviews? I'm not going to say hand on heart that I know this is a common practice, but I think yes, they probably do. There is very little follow up, and it's not that easy to check either way, although the proliferation of information on the internet now makes it slightly easier.

I was lucky enough to have Sky News use a clip of my show and a short interview for a piece on comedy at the Fringe. This was shown every hour for a whole day on Sky News (incidentally, despite being on national television all bloody day, it didn't lead to me selling ONE ticket on the back of it, so much for TV exposure), but after one of the pieces, they went live to the reporter on the Royal Mile who was interviewing Jimmy Carr.

At one point the interviewer, who was a lovely guy called Matt Smith (no, not the new Doctor Who), said to Jimmy in passing, "We went to see a good show last night by a guy called Charlie Ross."

Jimmy Carr immediately responded, "Oh yeah he's very good."

I know for a fact Jimmy has never seen my show, he's never met me and to my knowledge doesn't know anything about me. So I'm sure that he was being polite and respectful. Does this mean I can print on my posters,

".....very good..."
- Jimmy Carr, Sky TV, 2003

Nothing about that is untrue. But it would be disingenuous and a little fraudulent to use it. And now that I've written it here, I can never use it.

Reviews are generally like horoscopes, if it's a good one, you tell the world and believe it, if it's a bad one then you convince yourself the reviewer's an idiot with no clue and no taste and you ignore it.

Charlie Who?

Luck. Comes in two forms, good and bad. There are spells where you feel if you didn't have bad luck you'd just have no luck. Other times it feels like you just can't help landing on your feet. As my Mum used to say of those with blessed luck, "if he fell in the Clyde he'd come out with a fish supper in his mouth" (A "fish supper" being the Glasgow colloquialism for fish and chips).

Since as long as I can remember, I've loved a certain TV show, about a certain Time Lord.

To say that Doctor Who has played a major role in my life, would be like saying the Queen knows how to wave. So it will come as no surprise to learn that the eponymous twin-hearted hero features heavily in my stand-up. And after one particular night in May 2004, it was to feature rather heavily in my career.

I've already said that stage time is imperative, and that a comedian should strive to any gig. But what if you're ill? Is there a personal and social responsibility to abstain? Then there is a feeling that those who are self-employed just shouldn't – or don't – get sick.

This was a night like that. I was booked for a great little gig in London's Soho called Comedy Camp. It doesn't take a genius to work out that with a title like that, in Soho, that the tone of the night would be erring on the gay side. Now it is well known that Doctor Who is very popular in the gay community. I think the attraction, certainly to those of my generation who watched the show in the 70's and 80's, is that we were most likely drawn to a hero who wasn't sexualised, travelled, alone, an outcast from his own society, with beautiful women that he never showed any interest in – for all intents and purposes, they were the Doctor's fag hags - a term incidentally now replaced by fruit-fly, don't ask! – so, clearly on some sub-conscious, and more than likely fully conscious level, this was a hero that gay boys and men would find empathy with.

So on this evening when I was booked to do Comedy Camp, I had a cold and felt miserable. There is an unwritten rule in comedy that if you have to cancel, you try not to phone the promoter with a problem, but with a solution. I called around some other acts that I knew to try to get a replacement. None were available. Forced with the only choice of cancelling altogether or dragging my sorry ass along, do the gig and come straight home, I will forever be thankful that I chose the latter.

I was sharing the bill with the adorable Hattie Hayridge. I had first seen Hattie support Lee Evans on a tour in the 90's and instantly fallen in love with her style and her comedy. She had also starred in the cult comedy sci-fi Red Dwarf as Holly. Now the night had turned, Hattie was headlining and I desperately wanted to see her so I realised that far from getting home early, I was there for the night. Again, thank the heavens.

I went on, and given the nature of my audience, laid on the Doctor Who material. It went down well, and I had a lovely gig. The night went well, I stayed to watch Hattie, she naturally killed, had a great one (It's just occurred to me that if a comedian has a bad gig, it's a death, but if you do well, you killed. Wonder where the morbid and fatal motif came in? Has some poor comedian actually died after having a bad gig? Did a psychotic comedian have a great one then go on a rampage?).

Having a chat with Hattie afterwards, she said she was doing cabaret at a Doctor Who convention in Newcastle and had been asked to find a compère, would I do it? Of course, the answer was yes. That one moment was to irrevocably change the path of my career both in comedy, acting and writing. In fact if it were not for that moment, I wouldn't be writing this book!

Three months later, I was on my way to Newcastle. The company running the event is called 10th Planet Events (10th

Planet is the name of William Hartnell's final story as the Doctor, the first to introduce us to the Cybermen and the first to show the world the concept of regeneration when, at the end, Hartnell morphed into Patrick Troughton).

Now despite having been a life-long fan of the show, I had never been to a convention. I, like most people, had prejudices and a degree of reticence about such events. So I arrived at the hotel in the North-East of England. It was actually Stockton-on-Tees, a town not known as a tourist hot spot, and a casual wander up the High Street leaves with no doubts as to why. However, thanks to the good people at 10th Planet I was over the next few years to return to Stockton. In fact, here's a depressing thought, I've been to Stockton-On-Tees more than I've been to San Francisco!

That's depressing.

As I wandered around the various events at the convention I was struck by one major thing. Everyone was normal. Just like me. All sorts of men and women, young and old, wandering around, laughing at the bar, having a drink and generally just enjoying what was a very relaxing and warm atmosphere. Yes, there was the occasional fan dressed up in costume, but they were very much in the minority, and even that added to the occasion. There was a pride, a pride I had never been able to feel in being a Doctor Who fan. I felt better about the gig. But that was the next challenge. I kind of guessed that the audience weren't going to be hostile. I reckon if I had been challenged, heckled or even attacked on stage by a Doctor Who fan it would probably have made comedy history. But I had developed, added and tweaked my Who material, and here is the crux, the chance a comedian has to take when performing to a specific audience. A few questions were buzzing round my head.

Will they be too reverent? Will they be insulted that I'm mocking the show they love so much? Will they be comedy literate? Will anyone bother to show up?

For the first, I took the approach of emphasising that I was a fan as well. Hopefully endearing myself as "one of them" would help me not to look like another lazy comedian doing tired gags about wobbly sets and dodgy special effects. Plus, the fact that I had tailored the material to the theme of the weekend would hopefully demonstrate a degree of courtesy and commitment. You can never underestimate the advantage of a little preparation. If you go to a certain town, find out what the naff night club's called, are there any local celebrities, basically do your research, an audience always appreciates this in spades.

For the second, this is a problem for any event that may be corporate or organised outside the usual parameters that we would term as a "comedy club." Often, at these events, punters are there for another purpose and you can feel like you're just getting in the way. Many comedians have performed at corporate events where they were simply ignored by the audience, a thankless task, but usually a well-paid one. So you get on with it and take the money. It is one of those situations where if it goes well you take that on board, but if it doesn't, then it certainly shouldn't count towards your list of "deaths", unless of course you were on with other comedians and they all did well, then there is nobody else to blame.

As for the third question, well that's just fate. I was concerned that most people would, quite rightly, just want to sit in the bar, get pissed and talk about Doctor Who. I'm pretty sure if I were a paying convention punter that may be what I would want to do.

Well, I lucked out on all counts, they went for the Who-ribbing with great aplomb, if only in a "We can slag it off to each other but I wouldn't do this anywhere else" kind of way. They homed in on what was going on and were very appreciative that the organisers had bothered to put some cabaret on - and they turned up in droves. It was marvellous. Apart from one curious moment. I moved on from Who and wandered into my usual routine. At the point when I came out as gay there was a very definite split in the room. It seemed that about half loved it, and the other half had literally switched off. I asked someone later about that and he said, "Well, you have to remember that half the audience are gay, and the other half have just never had sex!"

After this gig I was hooked, I had made new friends, I had found kindred spirits and I was earning money as well. I wanted more. What was to follow changed me in ways that I cannot appreciate more. Over the course of the subsequent years I performed at many more conventions, as a result I was invited to appear in several Doctor Who audio adventures released by a company called Big Finish , on one playing a villain opposite Paul McGann, and another playing Rob Roy for Colin Baker's Doctor. Yes, I actually made it onto the show, albeit in a different medium, but what an amazing thing to do! At conventions I was given the honour of being asked to interview the guests on stage during the day, many of whom have become close friends (some readers will not be familiar but Who fans will, and I have to show my appreciation for the friendship and support given to me by Louise Jameson, Colin Baker, Frazer Hines, Anneke Wills, Sophie Aldred and Graeme Harper). And on that note, and probably more importantly than anything else, I have made some friends that will be in my life forever. All not bad for a gig I nearly didn't do.

It was three years later, as I was sitting next to Honor Blackman (yes, folks, Pussy Galore herself!) interviewing her on stage at a convention in Newcastle that I really started to pinch myself. It was on that day that, not only did Ms Blackman touch my knee (the most excited I've been about a woman in years), but she gave some prudent advice on how to name drop. I think she ascribes the skill to Lauren Bacall, and she says that in order to effectively name drop, you must place a light pause between the first and last name.

"So the other day I was talking to Bob (BEAT) De Niro..."
(Try it out loud, it works!)

It was at the self-same convention that I had the conspicuous honour of interviewing all the surviving actors who were companions to Patrick Troughton's second Doctor. Now by many fans of the show, Troughton's era is much-revered. For a start, it was the first time the character had changed, or to use the technical term for you Who-phobes out there, RE-GEN-E-RA-TED! If it didn't survive that, or to put it more bluntly, if Troughton didn't pull it off then the show was gone forever. Secondly, copies of most of the stories in Troughton's era are lost. Destroyed in the 70's in a moment of madness when TV executives thought that in the future, nobody would be interested in watching black and white television. The first Doctor's era was also affected but Troughton's was more or less savaged. It wasn't only Doctor Who that suffered, many episodes of Steptoe and Son, Dad's Army, Hancock, Peter Cook and Dudley Moore were also destroyed. Gone forever and consigned only to memory and in some cases, merely the audio track. Tragic. In fact, more than that, criminal. And ironic, given the success of Doctor Who DVD sales today. The BBC effectively destroyed a huge future income for themselves.

The five actors who accompanied Troughton, Frazer Hines (Jamie - the eponymous Highlander in the kilt, and now a good friend), Anneke Wills (Polly, also one of my closest Who friends and a wonderful inspiration to me), Wendy Padbury (Zoe, with whom I recently had the pleasure of working on a DW audio adventure, and who is a beautiful person) and the fabulous Deborah Watling (Victorian Victoria, charming, eccentric and tons and tons of fun). Missing was Michael Craze, who played sailor Ben. Michael sadly passed away a few years ago, but in recent years I have befriended his son Ben who works tirelessly to keep his father's memory alive, certainly amongst Who fans.

It is rare to get all of those actors together at the same event; they live in various parts of the country, and all are very busy, so to get them together on the same couch for an onstage interview is quite an achievement. So there was I, given the honour of chatting to them. Much of the conversation naturally gets drawn to the late and dearly missed Pat Troughton and of course Michael Craze. It is a touching, thoughtful and emotional interview. Frazer is tremendous fun and also a bit of a joker. Well, he thinks his jokes are funny, God love 'im! (Sorry Frazer, couldn't resist!) At the end of any panel, the floor is opened to the audience to ask questions. Attendees at Who conventions know each other and often some of the personalities that go gain a kind of fame of there own. One I am very fond of is Eddie, a guy from Glasgow who loves the show, naturally, and is rather distinctive. However, he is prone to getting a little flustered, particularly in the presence of his heroes. Now when Frazer was ten years old, he was directed in a film by a rather famous – no, I can go so far as to say an icon of the movies. Eddie wanted to ask what it was like to work with this icon, but in the pressure of the moment he crumbled. As I pointed to him to get him to ask a question he stuttered, "Frazer, what was it like when you were a child actor to work with (pause), eh (bigger pause) eh, (BIG pause) eh, what's his name?"

Frazer replies, "We're going to need a little bit more information than that, my friend!"

Eddie replies, the pressure of the moment is getting to him, "Eh, (PAUSE) och, you know, he was born on Christmas Day."

Frazer: "No, to my knowledge I never worked with Jesus."

The crowd are in stitches. I have to keep it moving as there is a forest of hands in the air wanting to ask questions. I politely asked Eddie to come back to us when he remembered. I ask for another question. Two questions later, someone is very politely asking something.

"Anneke, in the story The Highlanders was it very cold when you were filming in the…"

The poor man is interrupted as Eddie jumps to his feet and shouts, "CHARLIE CHAPLIN!"

The audience collapses in hysterics. How the hell can you forget Charlie Chaplin? Given that one of the people in front of him, on the bloody stage, he KNOWS is called CHARLIE!!!!

I love moments like that, and as we constantly see each other on the convention circuit, Eddie included, we continue to laugh about such moments. Great times.

So last year I was chatting to Sir Derek ... Jacobi ... (see what I did there?) and it was also in this meeting, again at a Doctor Who convention, that I came to realise something extraordinary about talent, and exceptional talent at that. In my time as a comedian, actor, Doctor Who convention person, I've met some very talented people, some very famous people (there is a distinction) and many in-between. It is at Doctor Who cons, however, that this is most prevalent. The actors I have encountered range from having played major roles in the show, villains, companions, the Doctor himself, to minor supporting roles. I have frequently found that those who often come to these cons with a dismissive attitude, a Billy-Big-Time if you will or as we'd say in Glasgow, "He thought he was all that an a bag o' chips," are those who don't really have the cojones to back it up. On the other hand, those like Colin Baker, Sylvester McCoy, Louise Jameson and the likes of Honor Blackman and Sir Derek Jacobi are the people I have met who have been utterly charming, approachable and as they say in the business, "old school," or in other words, class. And it reminds me of a phrase I heard many years ago and have always held close to me.

"Mediocrity knows no higher than itself, only true talent recognises genius."

I want to point out that I don't consider myself as the "true talent" or the "genius" in that phrase any more than I consider myself to be the "mediocrity," but it is wise to remember that in show business, and certainly in comedy specifically, success will only last as long as the laughs. In a gig, just because the previous joke worked doesn't mean the next ten will, and that is the same in a broader sense. To use a football phrase, you're only as good as your last game. The hit tour, or sell-out Fringe show only serves to pile on the pressure to meet those standards again. And that can be the downfall for success in comedy, which leads nicely onto the next chapter.

But going all the way back to that Tuesday with a cold and a gay gig in London... If I were to give any advice in this book, it would be this: go to every gig, even if you feel like shit in a handbag, do it. You never know what will happen.

Of course Doctor Who fans are a breed all to themselves. And like anything in life, there are extremes. Some fans just like watching the show, others take it very seriously.

The Comedy Closet

I'm a poof. Bender. Shirtlifter. Uphill Gardener. Queer.

There you go, I said it. Ah, you probably knew it! But it wasn't that easy to say at the start. For some reason, in the early days, despite some of my best material being about my sexuality and experiences I've had on many a gay scene, I found it difficult to perform this material to, for want of a better phrase, standard audiences. I had performed this material at gay and what is cutely described as "gay friendly" gigs, and naturally this material went down well. Although over the years, I and other gay comedians such as myself have found that to not always be the case.

From the start, I somehow had this weird notion in my head that if I started talking about my sexuality, I was running the risk of getting a punch in the face from someone in the audience. Now first, remember this was 2000. Although attitudes had moved on somewhat, the stink of Clause 28 was still in the air, it was the days before civil partnerships and even equal rights in the workplace. In a previous career, while I was a teacher of Physical Education, I had been appointed coach for the under-18's team at St. Mirren Football Club, a professional club based outside Glasgow in Love Street Stadium, Paisley. This was only 1998, yet when someone at the club discovered I was gay – to this day I have no idea how – I was summarily dismissed. Because of course, if you're gay then naturally all males of all ages are in immediate danger of molestation or even worse, conversion to the dark side. Because, as we all know, sexuality is something that is in flux and anyone can be turned gay under the appropriate hypnotic state (you get the training in hypnosis when you sign up!). I have always found it strange when people imply that somehow you can choose to be

53

gay. That one morning you simply wake up and think, "You know what, this woman malarkey, nah not for me, I'll give gay a go". Like the term "promoting homosexuality." What the hell is that? Can you just see the advert on television?

Is your apartment an unruly mess? Is your quiche pastry a little too soft? Are you tired of all that uncouth rock music and yearn for the tragic whinings of dead divas?

THEN WHY NOT TRY OUT THE GAY?

Yeah, it's nonsense. And of course there is the notion that being gay is unmanly. Well here you go for manliness. The then manager of St. Mirren was former player, and Scottish Cup winner, Tony Fitzpatrick. He had asked me to do the job, and seemed very pleased with the work I had done. Did he take me aside and tell me himself that I was to be given my marching orders? No, he got a volunteer who got £10 a week expenses to do it. Sadly he wasn't man enough to look me in the eye and discuss it. For the record, I have since spoken to quite a few of the lads I was responsible for, and they have told me to a man that they had no problem with my private life. It seems there is a generation coming through that we can be proud of.

So when I ventured into the comedy world, there was a bit of a hangover to this and all the "Keep the Clause" campaign backed by Scottish millionaire Brian Souter. A campaign so vile and disgusting, that it could only be compared to the open bigotry of 1930's Germany. Is that over-dramatic? Well, I would argue not. Imagine if you had red hair. And there were posters everywhere advocating that those with red hair weren't fit to teach, or to be trusted in positions of responsibility. That they were an element in society that had to be treated with caution. Imagine if those posters said this of people who were Jewish? Catholic? Black? Yes, when you change the term gay for any other group, then it takes on a much more sinister meaning. But what with homosexuality being – and to an extent this is still so – the last acceptable form of prejudice, there wasn't really much objection to it. On the very day I'm writing this, the 2009 winner of UK talent show, "The X Factor", Joe

McElderry, came out as gay. Now, this will come as no shock to almost anyone; he certainly came across that way on television, having, how can I put this, many of the classic "qualities" or character traits associated with being gay. I feel bad even writing that, as this makes the assertion that gay people can be spotted or recognised, which of course is very much not the case, but there does seem to be a percentage of gay people who fit this stereotype. And young Joe certainly came across that way. It's called a "gaydar", the ability to sense whether someone else may or may not be gay. Mine is shit, incidentally. Couldn't spot it a mile off. But others seem to have this ability.

Joe's first steps out of the closet have been met with apathy and that very attitude of "not surprised" or "does it matter?" Well, I think it does. There are still negative attitudes out there. Be they borne out of ignorance or religious beliefs, they do exist. So to have a young, successful, talented and good looking artist with a high profile coming out, then that can only be a good thing, and shouldn't be dismissed lightly. The very same attitude was applied to Ricky Martin, and again, this is important.

Genius writer and man who led the resurrection of "Doctor Who", Russell T Davies, said in his book "A Writer's Tale" that he was happy to be on the cover of the Daily Mail – a UK tabloid with a less than open-minded attitude to such issues – because it was an image of a successful gay man, and that can only be a positive thing to readers who may not be used to thinking of that from an alternative perspective.

Anyway, I digress. My point being that ten years ago, gays weren't the middle class acquisition they are today. And this made me very reticent about coming out on stage. I had a perception, and not an unjustified one, that audiences like gay humour, but they like their gays to be out there and upfront. As the greatest philosopher of our time Homer Simpson once said, "If you're gonna be gay, at least have the decency to mince around and make it clear, and stop calling yourself queer, that's our word for you."

I had this idea that it's all very well to compartmentalise a gay comedian as long as you could see what he or she was. But if someone is up there talking of football, pints and laddishness, then that brings it all a bit close to home. Could my mate be gay? Could I? To this end, I was reluctant to do it. Until one small gig at the Gilded Balloon in Edinburgh. Jill Peacock was the compère, and my great friend Scott Agnew was on as support. As I recall, I also think this was my first ever headline gig.

I was on great form and the gig was going well. Now the other issue of being a headliner is that you're expected to do a little longer than the support. As the gig went on, I realised I had to do more and was running out of non-gay stuff.

Fuck it. They seemed to like me. It was going well. A Dr. Pepper moment, what's the worst that can happen?

Of course, it was fine. I got a really good reaction, and an interesting one. And one that has continued to this day. The first part of my set is the usual stuff, yeah I'm just back from London and this happened, I used to be a PE teacher and that's funny because... etc, etc.

Then, about 10 minutes in, I do my big reveal. And it kind of is. In life, unless you signpost your homosexuality, most people will assume you're straight simply because that's what most people are. So in my case, the audience have subconsciously made up their mind. This guy is a straight guy. It's an automatic assumption. So when I come out, there is a tangible reaction. My friend and fellow comedian Ian Boldsworth, known on the circuit as Ray Peacock (and who also incidentally appeared in the episode of Doctor Who called "Blink," that many consider to be one of the best of all time) says that when he is on the bill with me, he likes to watch the audience just to see how they react. Now, in this day and age, a gay comedian is no big deal. Scott Agnew and Paul Sinha have no discernible quality that could earmark them as being gay, but they come out almost immediately and therefore the audience is given no time to make a decision, however unconscious that decision may be. Ian says they sometimes sit back in perfect synchronicity. It's a nice moment in the set, one I look forward to and I'm particularly proud of the way I do it.

In the beginning, for some reason I thought the reaction would be adverse, but aside from the occasional comment after a gig, which mostly comes in the form of, "Nice set mate, eh, don't think 'cause I'm talking to you I wanna shag you or anything!"

Which in a way is quite sweet. One of the worst reactions I've had was peculiarly after a gig at an HIV event with a predominantly gay audience. For a start, and this is strange, I have found, as has Scott Agnew, that the gays bizarrely like the camp, the drag and the flamboyant. I've always found performing for those audiences quite hard work. As if, because I like football more than Barbara Streisand, I am somehow betraying the cause. Actually I quite like Barbara, I've just never paid £200 to see her live. I once went on holiday to Gran Canaria, my mates told me how great the gay scene was in Playa Del Ingles. I went all excited and ready to party, party, party, only to find the entire place CLOSED! Ms Streisand was playing a concert in London and the entire gay scene had shut up shop to go see her. HONEST TO GOD!!!

There is one very good gay night I've played many times. The Comedy Camp is on a Tuesday night in London's Soho. It is an evening of comedy in the basement of a gay bar, aimed at a gay audience, billing gay or "gay-friendly" acts. I'm not quite sure what constitutes "gay-friendly," I often wonder if this is a protection phrase for the audience or the act. There are very few acts on the alternative circuit who do any directly homophobic material so surely most acts are gay-friendly. Unless there is a self-perpetuating myth here that gay audiences won't respond to a heterosexual male talking about sex with girls and going on about football. Audiences generally are more sophisticated these days, and frankly I don't think there's any act that wouldn't go down well with the predominantly gay audience. In fact, on one occasion I heard a brilliant opening line from the wonderful Ricky Grover. Ricky is an ex-boxer, known for his very hard image on stage, and is quite simply one of the best acts I've ever worked with. And a great guy to boot.

Ricky was booked for Comedy Camp one night I was on, and admitted to being a little bewildered, thinking his material may not work. I thought, and was right, that Ricky's act is funny in any environment, but he opened with a corker that set the tone perfectly.

As he menaced onto stage with the size and persona of Darth Vader on steroids, Ricky leaned over someone in the front row and says in a quiet tone, "Here mate, watch yourself, there's a few poofs in here tonight."

Naturally the audience warmed to him immediately, and he had a wonderful gig.

Being a gay act definitely gives you an angle. And that's important in stand-up. But less so these days. In fact, being an act with any kind of angle just means you have to find a fresh and different way of doing it. I have a background in sport, physical education and professional football, and that's kind of interesting. Just being gay in itself isn't. And there is always the danger that acts which have an angle will talk about similar things. Gay comics will default to coming out for example. And I know that I have a routine that Alan Carr also flies very close to, although has a fundamentally different joke at the end, so that makes us both different in that respect.

Someone said to me recently that being gay doesn't matter anymore. And I can kind of see that point. What she really meant was that it matters less. But it still matters. If that were the case, then you would go along to the Comedy Store tonight and you could see three gay acts on the same bill. However, this doesn't happen. You almost certainly *could* get three heterosexual males in their 30's talking about how bad they are at sex and what happens when their girlfriend gets her period.

Myself, Scott Agnew and Alan Carr would never be put on the same bill. We're all different acts, and generally talk about different things, and yet this would never happen. That's not because promoters are fundamentally homophobic. Far from it, most promoters are fantastically diverse, The Stand clubs in both Edinburgh and Glasgow have a policy of trying to, where possible, list a female act on any bill, and for many years had a regular gay and gay-friendly night. But there is still a feeling, and one that (to be honest) is perpetuated by gay acts including myself, that you don't want to "gay" the audience out. In fact, there is also a feeling among many of us that to have another gay act on the bill, takes our "thing" away from us. The "thing" that separates us from the rest of the evening. Audiences notoriously don't remember the names of acts they see on a bill, but I constantly have people remembering me as "the gay PE teacher." That's the ruthless selling point. Maybe the truth is, we – the gay acts – don't want the day to come when we can all be on the same bill. Maybe in some respects we want it to still *matter*.

But that's a selfish point.

It is true, audiences are more and more sophisticated, and a gay act is certainly no longer a shock or even a novelty. Yet there is still an incredible amount of ignorance about actual gay life. And that's what I try to do, and certainly what the best gay acts do. And if even one person leaves the gig with a even a slightly more positive view on homosexuality, then a large part of my job is done.

"Look, that's me on the telly!" – SUCCESS

Whenever I ask someone who is in comedy what they ultimately want to be, I like to hear, "to make as many people laugh as possible," "to be a finely tuned craftsman." What I don't like to hear, and often don't trust, is "I want to be famous."

Fame is a downside to the business. It really is. I'm not saying there isn't an upside, there are many, and the downsides aren't exactly a prison term either, but the point is, and I emphasise this as a comedian who is very definitely *not* famous, that the desire for fame itself will always detract from the quality of work that you do. Success, for a comedian, brings a range of pressures.

The first is a unique one to comedy. So you have developed, written and perfected up to an hour, maybe two, of exceptional material. Audiences lap it up, the shows are going well and the big time is around the corner. Now gigging comedians can live off the same body of work for many years. When doing a 20 minute set in a comedy club anywhere in the country, you can pick n' mix the stuff you feel like doing that night. It's a luxury to have that kind of space, to perform with freedom. Now that's not to say that I'm not constantly working on new stuff, but I have some great routines that I love doing, and have done for years. During a set I can't wait to hear the reaction, to see how it goes down, who likes it, who loves it and who loathes it. While performing, I actually get excited as I approach a favourite old routine, and during the telling of it am beside myself as I approach the punchline. And the upside to not being famous is that I can continue to do that week after week.

So then success comes along. A promoter or agent courts you, follows you and then decides that you will be the next big thing. You go on a major tour, you get slipped onto comedy panel shows on TV and BBC Radio 4, and then you get the pot of gold, a DVD release. Now all of this will undoubtedly make you money, depending on the level of sales, a lot of money, and that's all good and well. But once that material, that joke you've been plugging for years, that gag that has given you excitement and pleasure and entertained audiences for ages, once it's out there, that's it. It's gone. As I said in the opening chapter, comedians aren't like Elton John, we can't tour endlessly belting out "Your Song" till we drop. There is no such thing as a Greatest Hits for a comedian. The DVD release, the YouTube performance, the broadcast on TV, and that's it, gone.

So what next? Well you have to write new stuff. A whole hour, maybe more. Now that is a challenge that a comedian could, and should relish. But it is a source of phenomenal pressure as well. Your manager, agent or promoter will want to follow on from your success very quickly. A new tour to consolidate the success.

So what are the options? Well, the most talented will write a new show, and it will be great. Yes, some comedians can do that. Eddie Izzard produced at least four top notch shows with new material, any one of which would be worthy of any comedian writing in one lifetime. But even the greats can fall, and anyone who has seen Izzard's "Sexie" show will get what I'm saying.

The comedian one step down from the genius of the likes of Izzard has a few choices.

Now at this point you may be saying, but surely, Charlie, any comedian we see on TV or on a DVD *must* be as good as the likes of Eddie Izzard? Well, not necessarily. An awful lot of comedians out there will have short-term success, they are "of the moment" or the zeitgeist if you will. And it is called show*business*, those around them are there to make money. Again, nothing wrong with that, we're all in this to survive. But the pressure is now mounting. What do you do? Well of course you will write something, that's what we should be doing all the time. But with new tour dates booked and expectations high, you may wish to employ writers. Now taking on writers is a conundrum for the comedian. It's not only a case of finding someone who can write funny stuff, but can they write in your voice, in your rhythm, your meter. Once and only once did I use a writer. I teach a stand-up comedy class (see later chapter on that) and there was a great guy in it once, who was very funny. I thought, and still think, a very funny performer as well. But he decided that performance wasn't for him. I had an idea for a show I wanted to put on in the Glasgow Comedy Festival, but was struggling with a few aspects of it. I gave Andrew a brief for the show and asked him if he could come up with some ideas. He did. A lot of them were great. I loved them. Some I had to tweak to fit my style and the idea but generally, and because he is very gifted, they were good. However, in performance, they didn't really hit the mark, somehow I didn't deliver it with conviction and they didn't get the response I thought they deserved. I came to the conclusion that, for me certainly, it was a bit like wearing a second hand Armani suit. It still looks great, it still has quality woven through it, but ultimately it will never feel right because it's not yours, it wasn't made for you. It's for someone else. Again, though, that is for me. Many comedians use writers, I'm not going to name any here because they do go to great lengths to not let the public know they do, and that's fair enough. Some go to the point of using almost nothing but writers. There is one comedian, a young guy, who is getting a lot of TV appearances and moderate success at the moment. I was talking to the comedian who writes for him before the young comic was appearing on a TV panel show. After watching this appearance, I realised that every single word that came out of his mouth, had been written for him. There comes a point when you are no longer a comedian and become just a deliverer. You're getting paid for standing in the pub and telling your mates jokes you heard elsewhere. Not my style, and certainly not "old school." NO class.

So your success means that you're getting a second DVD. You have a new hour and a half to write. But where all your material from before was about life, old jobs, school, university, crap jobs, now you're a successful comedian. Your "life" consists of travelling from gig to gig, being pushed and pulled by promoters and agents, making TV appearances and going to Soho House or the Groucho Club because you can't really go to the pub anymore. Too many people hassle you, your old mates don't really fit any more because you have more money and you get to pull all the fit people that they fancy so there is a resentment, and even if there's not the general public won't give you and your pals any peace because they own you, and they are *obsessed* with celebrity so you have to make their day. Pose with them for a picture that will become the wallpaper on their iPhones, they want to talk to you and you have to oblige because they may come away thinking you're a tosser and if they tell ten people and those ten people tell ten people then that's potentially hundreds, maybe even thousands who won't buy your next DVD. So you ignore your mates and talk to Joe Public for half an hour. By then your mates want to move on, or go home. So you hang about with other successful people. And they are doing the same as you. So now the only experience you can draw on for comedy is a life of going from hotel to hotel, gigging and touring on a relentless road of monotony.

Two things. First, all of the above is from experiences that successful comedians have told me about. I'm sure there are idyllically happy, famous and rich comedians out there who have a great life and can continually write wonderful comedy. The point there is that the downside can make it very difficult and unpleasant.

Secondly, I'm not a bitter old tosser who wants to spit resentment at successful comics. I would gladly give any of the above a go to see what it's like, make the money and see what happens; it's partly what I do this for. Because, as many comedians have demonstrated, success can lead to other choices. But only if that's what you want or are capable of doing. Eddie Izzard has carved a very successful acting career out of his success, and know what? He's actually very good at it. Billy Connolly has become a successful travel pundit with many fabulous series combining his skill on stage with that of his charm and style in front of a camera and talking to people of the world. Jimmy Carr and namesake Alan Carr have trotted down the path of TV presenters and they are very good at that. So in order to be successful, there have to be other strings to your bow. And not everyone can do that. If you court controversy, then it's unlikely you'll have a long career in presenting, which tends to err towards the neutral, or likeable. There are exceptions but there are only so many formats that support this style.

Success for the stand-up comedian can be a mixed bag, you can make a lot of money but it can also have a hugely adverse impact on your career. Having said that, bring it the fuck on!

A Month in Edinburgh

August. Scotland's capital city. Usually raining. The Edinburgh International Fringe Festival is the biggest arts festival in the world. For three weeks in August, millions flock to a city that has limited capacity, no parking and an overstretched public transport system, purely to see comedy, plays, street performers, musicals, operas, anything that is going basically. There are thousands of shows to see, performed in established theatres, town halls, churches and any other available space. Seriously, ANY available space. Dark and drab basements of old Victorian buildings. old abandoned office spaces, back rooms of pubs and recently the inside of a double-decker bus! Anything.

The Fringe developed over 40 years ago as an alternative to the Edinburgh Festival, a high brow event focussing mainly on opera, classical music and theatre. The tickets for these shows are expensive and the audience considered elite.

The Fringe festival was open to all comers. Anyone can put on a show with no limitations or quality control. The punter takes their chances, are frequently disappointed, occasionally pleased and sometimes dazzled. The Fringe in its early days helped to launch the careers of Peter Cooke, Dudley Moore, Jonathan Miller, Alan Bennett (Beyond the Fringe), the Python team, Footlights…. Etc.

Now there's no getting away from the fact that a lot of the early Fringe success stories were Oxbridge alumni with well-bankrolled shows (probably paid for by Mummy and Daddy) and that is an aspect that continues to this day. There are plenty of venues filled with floppy haired public school kids destroying "Antigone" with over-indulgent foppishness to wring out one last pursuit of a career in the arts, get drunk and have sex before setting out on a career towards accountancy, high court judgery and general beigeness.

So how does it work?

Each venue has one or more – often a lot – of spaces to stage shows. The quality naturally ranges and there are big, well established venues. In no order whatsoever –

Gilded Balloon
C Venues
The Stand
Assembly Rooms
Pleasance
Underbelly

During the day, show times are split up throughout the day. Often starting as early as 9am and continuing into the early hours, split up into one-hour segments, sometimes longer.

Each show is allocated a time slot, and they will perform the show every day, in that time slot throughout the Fringe. This can be up to 24 nights, oftentimes shows will take one or two days off, some may do a limited run. Now I could fill pages and pages on the Fringe itself but I think it's more important to focus on what it has meant to me in terms of experience with, again, a few thoughts from other comedians.

I staged my first Fringe show in 2002. An opportunity came up to work under the banner of the Amused Moose. The Moose is a comedy club in London, run by the rather eccentric Hils Jago, and every year promotes and puts on shows at the Fringe. I managed to get a slot at the Underbelly, which at that time was an up-and-coming venue with a reputation for being edgy and exciting. The venue itself is in an unused building in Edinburgh's Cowgate, was dark, dank and probably a health and safety disaster, but had tons of atmosphere.

So how does it work? Well for starters, there is usually only one financial winner, and that is the venue. Now I'm not downplaying the fact that they take a chance, often on shows that are unseen, unwritten and on the back of random recommendations. But they are businessmen after all, and I'm not going to knock someone for generally trying to make a living. That's what I do, after all.

So what does the performer have to do? First, book a venue. Some of the bigger venues will ask for a reference, support from a promoter or even a copy of the show on DVD or audio. Smaller venues want their spaces filled so will be more amenable to negotiation. Venues may ask for a deposit up front, which will eventually be deducted from any profits made. On that note, a door split is negotiated between the performer and the venue. The nature of this is something of a power struggle. If you're a big name with the potential to sell out a show, then the performer holds all the cards, if that's not the case then the power shifts back to the venue.

The purpose of performing at the Fringe is usually not financial. It is an opportunity to be in the shop window. The downside being that it's a big window with a lot going on. Each comedian lives in the hope that they will be spotted by promoters, agents, television producers, virtually anyone with the power to advance their career. At the Fringe, these people are focussed, concentrated and available. But the odds? Very slim. There is a theory, and that is all it is, that most of these power brokers have already decided way before the August launch, which acts are going to be pushed and prodded towards success. Of course nobody would ever admit to this because then the majority of acts wouldn't bother paying what can be a considerable amount of money on a show that won't get anyone's attention. We kind of know this, yet we all still go. Why? Well for one thing, it can be a phenomenal experience. A chance to mix with many other comedians and performers, to network on a local level, make friends and, of course, party. Truth be told, that's a big incentive.

So what is the process?

Step One – Venue.

Finding a venue can be tricky. If the point of staging the show is to be seen, there are but a handful that will increase those odds considerably. Namely, one of the main venues I mentioned earlier in the chapter. Venues invite applications for shows early in the year, the usual procedure being to fill in the form, selecting the ideal room according to audience size and times. Afternoon gigs are difficult for comedy, but not impossible. Most comedians would opt for a time after 5pm at the earliest but ideally between 7pm and 10pm, later and the crowds become potentially more difficult to manage, but again better than 3 in the afternoon. The time slot and venue you get allocated will again depend on where you are in the power struggle previously mentioned. If you hold the cards then you'll get what you want, if not then the times could be tricky. Small venues are fine, in fact can be a bonus. It's much easier to achieve, and then claim, a "sell-out" show in a room for thirty people than in a one-hundred seater. With the large venues, you get the back-up of a larger marketing machine and the reputation. Edinburgh audiences are far more likely to take a chance on a name they're not familiar with, if it's in a larger venue.

Step Two – A show.

The next step is to come up with a show. At the Fringe it has become the thing, or even the norm, for a show to be a concept, or idea. Your show at this stage needs a title and a blurb (yes, that's the official term) giving an outline of what the audience can expect. This will also give the venue an idea so they can decide on whether to take your show on. This usually takes the form of a 30-50 word piece on the themes behind your show. This is still in the application process, so if you're lucky to have your show, or even parts of it on a recording of some kind then that will certainly help. As will any recommendations you can get from any other comics who have maybe performed at that venue before or who have a greater reputation than yourself.

Here is the "blurb" I used for one of my shows.

Charlie Ross – Tracksuits and Munchkins, C Venues, 2003

"Did Dorothy know the offside rule? Top Scots comic Charlie Ross takes off down his yellow brick road to discover what its like to be a butch guy in a camp world and love it!"

Short, to the point and trying to not give much away. If I were to, for example, use the word gay at any point, it runs the risk of immediately pigeon-holing the show, and taking away a good moment that is funny. There are, however, enough key words to grab some people's attention enough to get them in the door. Is that the kind of show you'd like to see? Well that's entirely up to you, and anyway you can't now as it's long gone, but that is the challenge you have. The most important thirty or so words of your comedy career.

Step Three – The brochure and marketing

Your venue has accepted you. You have maybe paid some money up front, maybe anything up to £500, or have negotiated a deal for an appropriate cut of the door money (remember all these financial bits and pieces, they're important!). Now you have to get your show into the Fringe brochure. This is a sizeable document – there are thousands of shows, and more or less EVERY one is advertised in the brochure – and you must pay for, at minimum, a 2cm by 6cm space to advertise your show. Most venues will insist on this, and that will be your blurb including prices, venue and show times. This small space will cost you in excess of £300 (are you counting this?). If you're particularly flush or just want to push for as much as advertising as possible, you can take out a larger advert in the brochure, the size of which can take the fee into the thousands.

The next stage is to design a poster and a flyer. If you're a genius on Photoshop or similar then this could drastically reduce your costs, but if you have to farm it out then design can be about £50-£100 if the designer is a mate. If not, then expect it to rise beyond that. Posters and flyers then have to be printed. Again, the venue will insist on this. During August, Edinburgh is awash with this stuff; in fact it's something of a tsunami of paper. Literally millions of posters and flyers, everywhere. I mean it. Walking down the Royal Mile is running the gauntlet of comedians, actors, musicians, street performers, all with something to sell, trying to convince you that their show is the one you must see today. Printers will usually give you a good deal on about 5,000 flyers and maybe 1,000 posters. The cost of printing in general has come down considerably in the last few years, so this could be around the £200 - £300 mark. But again, the quality may vary.

This is stage three, you haven't written one sentence of comedy yet and you're potentially looking at having forked out £1,200 at the top end, but certainly £800 minimum.

Step Four – Writing the show.

I have a chapter on writing a show, but as I said, it has become the norm for a Fringe show to have a theme of some kind. This has evolved out of what was formerly known as the Perrier award, now the Eddys (The Fringe comEDDY award), the judges of which felt that the comedian should be bringing more than just an hour or so of stand-up to the festival, but more of a structured show. I don't particularly agree with this. To me stand-up is fluid, organic and can't always be crowbarred into a structured concept. This can definitely work for some comedians, I just believe that there is a fine line between this being a comedy show, and a one-man play or performance. Fred Macaulay agrees, "This idea does restrict people; often they'll come up with a concept or a show title before they've even thought of writing anything. One of the best comedians and writers in the country is John Moloney, and he's never pandered to that. Year after year he just comes up with truly great stand-up."

I like comedians at their best when they are meandering from one idea to the next, often with few or no links, but just very funny comedy. Often the edginess of comedy is lost when the act tries to structure jokes around a theme, but that's just me, and only my opinion. Plenty of great acts have entertained thousands and done very well by doing this. What I do know is that when they go on the road and leave Edinburgh, that structure is often dropped. But hey, what do I know? Fred adds, "Once, I was tempted to write a show called 'Funny Just Isn't Enough' after a few years of doing very good shows and not getting a nomination. Although to this day I think a show I did with Lynn Ferguson had the best title ever, 'Fred Macaulay and Lynn Ferguson Do Some Stand-Up Comedy.'"

Step Five – Getting to Edinburgh

Yes folks, step four was the only one that didn't really involve forking out money, well aside from the time you spend on writing it, and maybe the coffees you buy if, like me, you can't work at home surrounded by loads of distractions. Now you have to actually go! If you plan to put on a show in the Edinburgh Fringe in the next five years, and it's really important to you, then I suggest that you move there! That way you won't have to fork out an extortionate amount of money on accommodation for the time that you're in the city. This can be extremely expensive. August is a month when a vast number of citizens moves away for the three weeks and lets out its flats for a small fortune. Be prepared to pay a lot, and be prepared to share. Think very carefully about the lifestyle you want to have when you're up there. If it's going to be party, party, party, then ensure that your flatmates will be thinking likewise, or else there will be conflict. And don't dismiss the party side. Socialising in Edinburgh is a vital part of the networking process. Everyone, and I mean everyone, is there. And getting to the right parties, the right private bars, the right mix of "biz" types is very important. Although it is very important to get the public in to see your show, getting TV producers, agents and promoters is equally important.

On that note, let's not forget that during your time there, all this socialising will cost you money. Oh, and occasionally you will have to eat. So we're at around £1,200 at the moment, and I reckon that's an average figure. I have been lucky enough to have a friend in Edinburgh I have rented from, and even based on "mates' rates" that was £300 for the three weeks. So add that on. Booze and food, well everyone differs on that one. But let's say that you could shift £100 a week on that, easy! That's you up to around the £1,800 - £2,000 mark. Now you have to sell tickets. No, I mean you *have* to sell tickets! Unless you can afford to piss the best part of £2k up a wall on the lottery that someone will discover you, and I know some people can, then fine. If not, then you have to recoup some of your outlays. So now the work begins.

The show is written. The posters and flyers have been delivered. The venue space is available. Good to go.

The first three days of the Fringe are often preview days, ticket sales are on a 2 for 1 basis and it's understood that this is a "bedding in" period. That's not to say that your show won't be reviewed or that audiences won't expect something with quality or substance. The day before you will get time to tech, this is to run through any technical aspects of the show you may have. There is often only about a 20 minute turnaround between shows so you have to be prepped not only to set up your show but to clear it almost as soon as the last audience member's arse has left the seat. So the best approach is minimalist. The show before or after you may be a play with a lot to set up, so it adds more stress if they or you hang about and don't get sorted quickly. So the tech is vital not only to set up, but to get to know the acts before or after you.

Most comedy shows are straightforward, a microphone, a stand and maybe some intro and exit music.

So after the tech is cleared, you're good to go. Then the nightmare begins. Not the show. That will become the easy part of your day. The nightmare is promotion. In other words, flyering.

If you've been off the mark, you will have got yourself to Edinburgh early (or at the very least arranged for someone else to get there), and put up as many of your posters all over the place as possible. Even this isn't that easy. Naturally you can poster as much as you want in your venue. But many walls and billboards have been bought over by promotions companies, so there are many places it's absolutely forbidden to put up your posters. There is no point putting them up anyway, given that your bloody name and an easy time and location to find you are plastered all over the thing. They will find you, and it won't be pleasant. If you arrive at the same time as everyone else, then the experience will be akin to trying to get a seat on a train that is the last one of the day, and the previous six have been cancelled. Horrific. Thousands of performers, remember plays will have a large number of cast members to spread around. As is the way in the world of the comedian, you will probably be on your own. So you have your posters up wherever you can that is going to be prominent and will not get someone busting into your show with a baseball bat to break your legs, then that's done.

Flyering is a soul destroying process. Basically you will spend most of your day leading up to your show, wandering up and down the Royal Mile in Edinburgh trying to thrust your flyer into the hands of as many people as possible – their hands may already be full of flyers for other shows – in the hope that something you say or something that's on your flyers will convince them that your show is the one they should see that day. Of course a large number of people will ditch your flyer in a waste bin as soon as they are out of sight of you, some may even just do it metres away from you. Plus, as comedians, we

73

have the indignity of selling ourselves. This begs one major question.

"If you're that good, then why are you out here doing this for yourself?"

And here is the next financial dilemma. Paying someone to do it for you. How much does that cost? Well, depends on who you get. Students will sometimes work for buttons to get some Fringe experience and extra beer money, the other alternative is to use some of the many professional marketing teams that are trawling the streets.

Of course the easiest way to do all this is to have your show produced and promoted by one of the big agencies – Avalon, or Off the Kerb. To name a few. The advantage is that the whole package comes as one. Design, printing, promotion, venue and marketing. The machine gets behind you and all you have to worry about is your show, that is the way it should be. Of course the cost is end loaded and often pretty hefty, and anyway, to get promoted by one of these guys is usually an invitation only scenario.

A cynic or conspiracy theorist could of course suggest that the whole thing is a massive arrangement between venues and printers to build as much business as possible.

Here is a big question: Does flyering work?

I have written and performed three Fringe shows to date. I occasionally in my shows do a straw poll. I ask my audience, "Who came here today as the result of a flyer?" The percentages, I have to say, are often very low. I mean, LOW. Certainly below the 5% mark. There has also been research that suggests that around 80% of flyers are on the ground or in a bin within 30, yes THIRTY, seconds of receiving it. And at best they go home in a pocket and end up binned anyway. I am convinced that flyers work within a venue, if someone wanders into your venue looking for a show to go to, then they will seek the flyer out as they are sure to be lying about on the bar, on stands or at the ticket and information area. As for standing in the rain on the Royal Mile indiscriminately handing out these bits of paper, I'm not so sure. So, why do it? Well because everyone else does, silly. Or is it that I'm just very bad at it? That could be the answer, but my numbers have often been good, and in one case, I made a small profit. So what does bring punters in? Fred Macaulay says in the mid-90's he never flyered.

"I would get 400 posters and that's it. For me it was always word of mouth that was the most important thing. But now, marketing is crucial, so I'm not sure you'd get away with just that now."

Being in the brochure is a must, absolutely.
Poster - get your face seen prominently.
Performing in one of the big venues gives a certain kudos.
Reviews.
Reviews.
Imaginative publicity.
Reviews.
Any TV/radio exposure you can get.
Oh, and did I mention? Reviews.

Ironically, you generally only get TV exposure if you have a sell-out show. In other words if you're a big name. The big guns will sit on a nice studio couch, and will chat away to some beige TV presenter about their show and how good it is, what they will be talking about. And amuse you with witty and urbane comments. The beige TV presenter will ask said comedy celeb where and when we can see their show, and much to every grafting non-famous comedians bewilderment, the answer is, probably on tour in about six months. Most of the hundreds, possibly thousands of comedians out there on the Royal Mile with a bunch of flyers in their hands would kill to have any kind of media publicity and most definitely a bit of TV exposure. And here is where I come back to the spirit of the Fringe. By its very nature, if you *can* sell out a show in

Edinburgh in August, then you could probably sell out that show at any other time in the year.

A £20 ticket to see, for example, Ricky Gervais equates to almost **THREE** other shows of comedians that may well be fantastic and you won't get to see on a tour or a DVD. People who are fans of Ricky Gervais will probably pay £20 to go see him at any other time of the year, so here is the question.

Why are you cutting our grass, Ricky?

Sandy Nelson adds, *"It has become too big and cut-throat for my liking, and full of chancers who concentrate more on their hobnobbing than on their show."*

Of course it's not just you, Ricky, but everyone else who is a big name who does the Fringe... Get the hell out! I can say, hand on heart, that I wouldn't be seen within a country mile of the Fringe if I could sell out a run in advance. That's so not what the Fringe is for. Well, certainly not what my interpretation of the Fringe is for. The second you're selling out, you're mainstream, you're NOT "fringe."

Of course, it's possibly not down to Mr Gervais, it is the same marketing sensibility that puts comedians in the totally inappropriate arena gig, that sends major acts to the Fringe. MONEY. These guys tend not to care that the next big thing, or even next mediocre thing, is out there putting blood and guts into a show that nobody of any significance will see. They want to grab as much moola as they can.

I'm not totally out of touch with that. Again, it is show*business*.

But creativity requires breathing space, and if the struggling acts are going to be crowded out by costs, overheads and all in some futile gesture, then simply, less and less will do it. And some may say that's a good thing. The Fringe could possibly do with less shows, and certainly less comedy. But talent, genuine talent will get lost. And that's shameful.

Now. You may be thinking that these are the bitter ravings of a failed comedian who has never cut it, or hasn't made any kind of impact at the Fringe. That may be somewhat true. So here's the evidence.

I have written and staged three Fringe shows.

Charlie's Angles – Underbelly (2002)
Tracksuits and Munchkins – C Venue (2003)
Just One Word – The Beehive (2008)

In my first show I made a small profit, audiences were good, and I got several reviews. None less than a 3-star and two 5-star. That's not bad at all.

The second had less successful audiences, despite, bizarrely, as I mentioned in an earlier chapter, a whole day of promotion in an interview on Sky News every hour. But again, reviews were favourable, again none less than 3-star and one 5-star.

The third was slightly different. As part of the Free Fringe, it was a great idea but not supported by reviewers. Only two reviews, one 3-star and one 4-star.

Now, out of three Fringe shows, that's not a bad batting average. Generally favourable reviews. Generally well attended. Any impact on my career at all? None. Apart from the chalkface benefit that working every night for 23 nights makes you sharp as a tack performance-wise. You can see why I took 5 years off.

I came back to Edinburgh in 2008 to perform at the Free Fringe. A brilliant idea of playing in venues, in a non-ticketed show, and at the end the audience has a choice whether to leave some money in a bucket at their own discretion depending on whether they have enjoyed the show, or at the very least liked you enough to pity you. Kind of like busking indoors. I travelled through from Glasgow every day to keep overheads down, and really was quite happy if I made my petrol and poster money back. In fact, I did. The show was great fun to do and I had a great Fringe experience. Sadly, the media's attention and imagination wasn't caught by the concept. It was generally believed that, to quote my 4-star review: *"It's the Free Fringe, this can't be any good can it?"*

Although the very same review did go on to say, *"Actually this was one of the best shows I've seen this year!"*

And that was the problem. There were loads of great shows from fabulous comedians in the Free Fringe, but sadly not one big act took part. That is what it needed. Stewart Lee did support it and said that he would not be averse to performing at the Free Fringe, for if anything held the spirit of the Fringe true to its heart, it was this. I lost no money, I enjoyed the experience and really, if truth be told, it made no more or less impact on my career than the previous two, more official, shows.

So where were we on the cash ready reckoner, about £2,000 I think. So your show is selling ok, audiences are up and down, and lets say you get some favourable reviews. Now you are in a city that has some of the most influential people in your business kicking about, and reasonably accessible.

How do you access them? Well you go to parties, events, hang around the venue bars, if you can get a ticket to the performer-only or VIP bars, even better. That way, you never know who you'll meet. So when you're in a bar or at a party, what do you do? Well you have a drink. Now if you are completely professional and focussed then you will make the Fringe experience a dry one. Staying sober is a surefire way to get the best out of the experience, to ensure that your performances are as close to top notch as you can get, and keep your mind on task. It also means you're less likely to make a total tit of yourself when you get out there to network. Of course, an incredible number of us fail miserably at this. My best networking was done at my last show, where I chose to drive through to the show every day from Glasgow, so obviously I wasn't drinking, the irony being that any promoters I spoke to had a blank expression every time I mentioned the words "free" and "Fringe" in that order. Then came the long explanation about this being a statement, which again falls on deaf ears as most of their acts are doing shows in the main venues. So, a bit of an own goal there. Again, a lesson learned.

I don't generally find networking easy. Just talking to people about how wonderful you are is a difficult task, very few can pull it off successfully. Think of it, how can you try to sell your act without sounding arrogant and full of yourself, and come across as the kind of guy that a promoter would want to work with? Well having a wingman is good. Someone who can do the icky bits for you. Getting promoters and reviewers to your show is also vital. That part is relatively easy to ask as that's what everyone is doing, but then you have the problem that, if these guys are getting invited to twenty or more shows a day, you have to make yours stand out. How?

All this socialising naturally costs more money, and during festival time, Edinburgh ain't cheap. It generally isn't the cheapest city anyway, but as you can imagine, when over two million people are converging on your city, it is a chance for businesses to clean up. Quite rightly so. So the money you will have to spend on drinks and food has to be factored in as well. Now nobody could, or should, survive 24 nights out in a row, although many do try! But consider partying or socialising about 15 nights in total. A quiet night could be about £30, a big night well, anything in excess of £60 can be spent easily. Most venues do give discounts to performers, but the discount, although very much appreciated is modest and is still usually above normal bar prices. So let's average those two figures out to £40 a night, over 15 nights out, well ok, let's assume not everyone is a drink obsessed party goer, lets make it 10, that still factors in another £400. So where were we? About £1,800 - £2,000? So that take us to £2,200 minimum, and remember, I've been reasonably conservative here. This is based on a small show, in a small venue, with basic shared accommodation, eating minimally and socialising on a shoestring. None of which is easy at the Fringe because there is so much going on, it's easy to get lured into the excesses of what's going on around you. Now don't forget you're already paying your usual bills, rent where you live etc, and that has to be considered as well.

In fact, the really bad news is I have been VERY conservative. In his book Stewart Lee reckons the average cost of a Fringe show is, wait for it, £7,500! Now I do think, in fact I know it can be done cheaper. I know this because I've done it cheaper, I so don't have £7,500 to spare and yet I've staged three Fringe shows.

So there is certainly a random element to Edinburgh. Most comedians do it because, well everyone else is doing it. Is there an alternative? Stu-Who? has an interesting theory.

"I've been saying for years that a better way of spending your £7,000 is to book a major London venue. Invite as many TV producers, agents and promoters as you can. Set aside money and promise free drink. As they come in, give them a bag of cocaine, and employ some call-girls (or call-boys?) to keep them entertained. Do your show to a captive audience, the show they would basically have seen in Edinburgh but are never actually going to come to. I swear if you can't get a TV deal out of that then you wanna chuck it."

Stu has his tongue slightly in his cheek, but the more I think about it, it may not be such a bad idea. Any business advisor would tell you that is a much more efficient use of resources than placing yourself in a market where you are immediately competing with over a thousand other acts who are doing exactly what you are doing.

However, there is a school of thought that all of those TV producers, agents and promoters want to see that you can do a Fringe run, that you can maintain the funny over 24 nights and sustain a high level of critical acclaim. So there's the dilemma.

I've sounded very, well, down on the whole experience. I don't mean to. I've found each experience different, I've made loads of good friends, tons of contacts, and at the very least, got an awful lot of general gig work from doing it. There is a reality about it all though, and the point I suppose I want to really make is, be selective. Don't be in a rush to get there, and don't just do it because everyone else is. There is, however, one thing to remember about the whole experience. It's hard work, can be depressing and as we've seen, very depressing.

But, it is fucking brilliant!

Writing!

So as I said in the section on material, there are many and varied opportunities to get things that can be transformed into a comedy routine on stage. As I am writing this, the Glasgow Comedy Festival is fast approaching. This year will be my seventh show. Last year was less than good, I had left the show too late to write so it ended up being a mish-mash of ideas peppered with old, tried and tested material. There was also a technical element to the show which due to a series of unforeseen circumstances went horribly wrong. This year it's going to be different. And you're going to accompany me.

This is the one part of the book that will go right to the heart of writing a show. Material in it's earliest form will be out there, so if you don't want to know the trick, or the smoke and mirrors, then you may not want to read this section. But basically, we're about to write a comedy show…. Let's see what happens.

So this is a comedy festival. I've left it really late to organise it. The deadline for getting into the festival officially, which includes an advert in the brochure, is early November and it's the 25th of October. I have nothing. No venue. No idea. No clue.

At last year's festival I had got my fingers slightly burnt. The previous three shows had packed out small venues, and on the two occasions, people had been turned away. So that was an estimate of around 150 people coming to see me regularly. In 2009, I had gone out on a limb and had hired a small theatre space and would put on two shows. The two show idea made no difference to me financially as they were both on the same night, and the first show would, if quiet, work as a rehearsal.

Of course, with the usual irony of performance, the audience I had built up over four years deserted me in droves. Technical issues prevented the first show from going ahead, and the stresses and strains took their toll. It was poor. Money was lost. The Magners Glasgow International Comedy Festival 2009 was one to be forgotten. Certainly by the public, not by me.

2010. A new decade, a new start. I would not be caught out again.

Or would I? The 25th October passed. As did the 26th, 27th and the 28th. On the 29th I remembered about a small group of comedy promoters who had booked up some small venues and were putting on shows. They are called The Go Button. Basically two lads who had done a marketing degree and loved comedy, initially running a good little gig in Glasgow for new acts. I gave Graeme Mackay a call.

They had a slot I could fill (Given what this show is to become, that line will very soon take on a new meaning!). *Venue: Capitol, Sauchiehall Street.*

I was very aware of the venue, having played a gig there before, and having been to some functions in it. Lovely room, perfect for comedy and had all that I needed.
Date: Friday 12th March at 8pm.

Good time, nice date. Saturdays are often better, but as it turns out the next day is the Scotland v England rugby match. So a let-off there.

Now for some financial ins and outs. The deal.

There would be a 70/30 split of profits. Now this would to some – particularly actors – seem quite high. Well I had to consider a few things. The Go Button guys had a good reputation for working hard on promotion. They would sort the posters, flyers and brochure entry. And they also are known to work very hard to promote the show. I'm working on the premise that, the more tickets are sold, the more money they will make. This may seem obvious to you, but it's a simple formula that is lost on an awful lot of promoters. On one

83

occasion a promoter I had signed up to put out his own brochure for his company's gigs in the comedy festival, as well as the main one. Despite agreeing a 60/40 cut! (What was I thinking?) My show failed to appear in his own bloody brochure! He was sacked. Thankfully I sold out anyway. That year I got 100%.

This year, I'm less sure. Confidence has been shaken by last years events and I feel I need to focus entirely on the show and not anything else.

However here is the curious thing about marketing.

In 2009 I hired out a small theatre space that was:

a) doing shows in the comedy festival – an established venue

b) a very well respected venue, in Glasgow anyway

c) had a mailing list of over 3,000

d) had a full-on poster campaign.

To break even, I only had to sell a total of 130 tickets over two shows. Based on previous years, this seemed very do-able.

I ended up having to pay THEM £90!

Marketing is curious. There are no guarantees.

So this year, I've gone smaller with less financial outlay and a more vibrant and imaginative campaign.

So now that the business side is done, where do we begin? I need a name for the show. As the deadline is 5th November and I need some blurb (that's the official term) about the show to go into the brochure.

Now I've already explained about "concept" or "themed" shows in the Fringe. I know I don't really like the idea, or I do, as long as it's a really good idea. How often does that happen? It's the 3rd now and I'm not likely to come up with a great idea in that time frame. So CHARLIE ROSS LIVE it is then!

On the 4th of November one of these curious things happens. Is it the big God of Theatre as I've mentioned elsewhere? Is it luck? Fate? Who knows.

I switch on the TV, and for some reason, I have been watching ITV3 the night before. I rarely watch anything on ITV, especially now that the joyous "Kingdom" starring Stephen Fry has been cancelled, but the night before I chanced onto a James Bond film. Does anyone else do this? I love Bond, a really big fan. I have ALL the DVD's in special edition copied and beautifully restored in surround sound in full widescreen. And yet, that night, when I saw "The Spy Who Loved Me" (one of the superior 007 movies and easily Moore's best) on the guide for ITV3, did I get up and put on my wonderful DVD copy? No. I watched it on the telly for about an hour. I fell asleep. I switched the TV off. ITV3 was still on.

The next evening I put on the telly for the first time that day, ITV3 is showing "Carry On Screaming." Another DVD I have, but I make a cup of tea, open a packet of chocolate hob-nobs and sit down to watch this comedic feast, pain in the arse adverts and all.

As Kenneth Williams utters his final lines "Frying tonight!" it occurs to me. I love camp humour. I always have. In fact, doesn't everyone? Or do they? Is it a dead form of comedy, consigned to nostalgia and a more innocent age? That's enough internal questions to start sketching something out. The ideas are now whizzing round my mind, time to reach for a pad and start to throw up these thoughts onto paper.

Look at what's popular now. This was the first line research. Paul O'Grady. Graham Norton, Alan Carr. All extremely popular, current, contemporary, and camp as the proverbial row of big pink tents.

This is going somewhere. I love, and I mean really LOVE, that comedy. It's never really gone away, Britain loves it. And the very fact that I'm watching an old camp piece of nonsense on television at 7pm is proof enough in itself.

A show about camp humour. Not necessarily a camp show. Just looking at camp comedy. Why? I had always had the notion that mainstream audiences – ah fuck it, let's call a spade a spade – STRAIGHT audiences – who love camp comedy, and seem to accept that level of homosexuality quite readily but less so on their doorstep, was because most camp comedians are desexualised. We can't see Larry Grayson, John Inman, or even Alan Carr as sexual beings. That's the key.

Now I'm excited. This is a show. It's interesting. Potentially very funny, as I know I have a captive audience that loves camp humour, and I can play around with the ideas. Plus, I'm motivated, I'm excited, and that's the best part of all.

But what to call it? It took about five seconds to come up with:

"CARRY ON CAMPING!"

In a sense, I'm playing around with the words in almost exactly the same way as they did way back in 1969.

And then in about ten minutes, I come up with this, THE BLURB!

Charlie Ross - Carry On Camping!
Ooh missus, no really, shut yer face and listen up. Us Brits really do like a camp titter don't we? Whether its innuendo or upyerendo, you can't beat a good old fashioned pussy gag, and the very not camp Charlie Ross wants to find out why. So he's filling a big slot at Capitol and going to give you all a big one. So stop messin' about, and we'll all be laughin'!

So there you go. The foundation for a show. And that's really all it is at the moment. The hard part is about to come. Writing the bloody thing.

Where do you start? Well, for me, the first place is kind of to write down what you want to say. Is there a point to be made? Or are you just going to stand there telling knob gags and spouting innuendo for an hour? The answer to that is definitely no. Ok, so I want to make several points:

86

Why do we Brits love camp comedy?
What is its history?
Is the 21ˢᵗ century equipped for it, now we can say what the old school camp comedians could only imply?
Is there a serious undercurrent of homophobia here?
Straight guys feel more secure with camp gay guys, they know where they stand.

These ideas will stay there. They float about. The minute you get bogged down in philosophy, it's easy to get lost and the project becomes a one-man show. So this is actually the way I see that list.

Why do we Brits love camp comedy?
MAKE IT FUNNY!
What is it's history?
MAKE IT FUNNY!
Is the 21ˢᵗ century equipped for it, now we can say what the old school camp comedians could only imply?
MAKE IT FUNNY!
Is there a serious undercurrent to homophobia here?
MAKE IT FUNNY!
Straight guys feel more secure with camp gay guys, they know where they stand.
MAKE IT REALLY FUCKIN FUNNY!!!

One, or all of these ideas will go if I can't get the line in bold to apply. That is what makes it a stand-up comedy show. A one-man show is a monologue that *can* be funny, in fact, it can be very funny, but if you go too far down the path of wanting to make a point, then it's very easy to get lost!

The next stage is to look at what I already have. Some of the ideas I'm already performing may apply here. In fact, I already know a few do, but this is an opportunity to expand them.

Equally, I know that the majority of my usual stand-up will be ditched.

The first major decision is simple. In my current stand up, I take pride in one moment. It's the moment, usually about 10 minutes in where I've been rambling on about reality TV and what it was like to be a PE teacher, with lots of nice stories about school kids and being a sporty Scottish guy. Up to that point, in the audience's sub-conscious, I'm another straight lad. Then, WHAM! I come out as a trumpet blowing homo! As I've mentioned before, comedian and mate Ray Peacock always comments to me that he likes watching the audience at that point. There is almost a sharp intake of breath in unison. Now this isn't because I'm gay. Maybe it was ten years ago, now the gay thing on its own is nothing special, it's that audience has made up its mind about me. They have slipped into a comfort zone, and they just don't see it coming.

Interestingly, as I type this, I am thinking that, this in itself may be something worth talking about in "Carry On Camping."

So my first major decision is that I have to come out a lot earlier in the show. The last thing I want to come across as is a gay bashing straight comedian.

Again, bizarrely, as I type this, maybe that is EXACTLY how I should come across! Now here you are, this is happening in real time, as I'm typing this, the process of writing is going on, and if you could see me, you would note that I am flicking between screens, the one that has the title "Carry On Camping" and the one called "A Comedian's Tale," one process is feeding into the other. **Note to self: Must make sure to tell the editor that this section must at all costs remain intact, this is fluid!**

Anyway, whatever I decide, it's going to be a lot easier to get to the heart of the camp humour if I come out earlier. That way I am free to explore these ideas without being judged.

So what do I have? Well there is a nice story about an air steward I slept with who came up with a lovely example of camp humour that well and truly put me in my place. Another story from a Virgin records store in New York that involves three straight girls, which will show breadth. Camp isn't always about the gay. Both stories have the opportunity to expand. This is good. I need a list.

I have an iPhone. Ok sorry, there, I've said it. For many this device seems to be the official sponsor of posing wankers recently, but I love mine. For me as a comedian, it has two vital components.

A notes facility and a voice recorder. The latter is brilliant in that, because it's a phone, you can walk along the street spewing ideas with comic potential and still look like your on the phone. The old days of talking into a dictaphone and looking like a tit are gone. The notes facility has replaced the pad and pencil I used to carry everywhere in case I saw or heard something I had to talk about. Comedian and Radio Clyde One presenter Des Mclean who has played three sell-out shows at the Clyde Auditorium in Glasgow emphasises how important this is.

"I used to go about saying I never write anything down, but that's bullshit. I carry a notepad everywhere, cos you never know when and where your going to see comedy. On the bus, in the pub, sitting on the toilet. I'm old fashioned, I like to use and actual pen and paper, so I carry a little notebook with me everywhere. The most invaluable tool to comedy I have."

Just don't lose that notepad, Des!

So a list is in order. This is something that basically, you put anything and everything down on. Keeping it brief, bullet points, BUT in such a way as to make it clear to you. There is a folly in this plan...

Here is the list as it stands on 2nd February 2010:

Carry on camping.
It's Levine,
Madonna in hospital,
You think that's wise,
We're not expecting grandchildren,
Optimistic camp Americans- Judy Garland alive and well,
Stylophone,
Phobias,
Psychology of camp,
DICC,
Gay detector avoidance, talk about girls all the time,
Margoyles / Di Caprio,
The Whiffenpoofs,
Von Trapps most famous Austrian family till Josef Fritzl,
baroness being a cow,
Chicken soup,
Singles box & Desert Island Discs,
Gangsta hand gestures Bond villain palsy,
Psychological Facebook,
If he gets me a cap for Scotland he can suck my cock- St
Mirren,
Ashley's been fired in Virgin,
Rubbish/trash,
Camp guys on telly who weren't gay or didn't talk about it...
Desexualized.
Camp Nazis,
Fox hunting stuff.....remember that?? *Lol*
Straight acting.

Now a lot if not all of this stuff will mean nothing to you. In
fact, it shouldn't. Well some of it you get the idea, but the
comedic potential is in my head, they are prompts to remind
me or guide me to where I thought of it. Now I don't expect
that in performance it will actually be as written on the page,

but the structure has to be there. I feel it's vital in this instance to get the shape right. Remember...

MAKE IT FUNNY!

If I can't do that then it will get ditched. For example. The Whiffenpoofs are an all male singing group made up of undergraduate students from Yale university. They sing songs like "Mr Sandman," are all very old school, all young, often very handsome men, and the name has the word "poof" in it. This is a show by a gay man about camp humour. If that idea isn't at least worth exploring then I don't know what is. I just don't know yet. Maybe we'll find out along the way. It's a "parachute routine", I just haven't found the funny yet, but I know it's there! There are a few routes here. I might just put out all the words on a page.

Whiffenpoof
All boys
Yales
Fresh Faces
Old songs – titles?
Virginal

And so on, it's nothing more complex than word association. See where that takes me. Look for a play on any words, double meanings, double entendre, anything that could be used for comic effect.

Then I may look into some research, any scandals, stories about the Whiffenpoofs themselves, history, look on YouTube for any footage that may prompt an idea.

The last resort is to sit down with friends or a comedy mate. This is not a last resort like a desperate attempt to drag something out of the idea, my mates are way too funny for that. But I like to try all avenues and possibilities myself. Using writers is something I've rarely done. I don't know, I always feel that I want to stand and fall by my own words. I did ask a very talented guy I met who had little interest in performing. But boy could he write. And the stuff he wrote for me was good. But I was asking him to write to my brief, and for my voice. When I tried it out on stage, it just felt uncomfortable. Like wearing someone else's jeans that don't quite fit. Does the job, but you're dying to get them off and put your own on. I know a lot of performers use writers, and I'm sure it works for many of them, and I'm not saying that one day I won't. If you're using writers it means you're successful! But I'm pretty certain that Billy Connolly, Eddie Izzard and Woody Allen (to name but a few – essentially, my heroes) never used writers at any time. Sometimes that shows, but when they get it right, they are invariably better than anyone else. That's what I aspire to. Maybe I won't achieve it, but if you're aiming for perfection, then at least what you come up with will be very good.

I have my list. I'll probably keep adding to it right up until the week of the performance. Things can be added. I've written about four pages of prose so far. Not sure what that equates to in actual time. There is some physical stuff in there. It's the second of February and I'm compèring the new act/material night at The Stand in Glasgow tonight so there will be an opportunity to try some stuff out there. That is the next step. Often if you go to these new act nights, you will find experienced acts, and sometimes very famous ones, trying out some material for a new show, tour or TV show. So take the chance, you never know. Plus a lot of new acts are quite good as well. They are a very good way of seeing people in the early stages of a comedy career, however long or short that may be.

So what have I written?

As I've already said, this is the first time I've written something in its entirety. I've always worked off bullet points in the hope that it will always sound as if I'm just saying things off the cuff. But in this show, the language has to be specific in a lot of the routines. One of the great camp comedy performers, Frankie Howerd, was famous for his "Ooh missus" and "Titter ye not" catch phrases. Not many knew that every "Ah," "Oooh missus" and "Shut yer face" was scripted to the nth degree. He was meticulous in his writing. Now, I absolutely don't want this show to be like that, but I do want the words and the language to play their part, and that requires careful planning.

The big problem with seeing things written down is that they never read as being that funny. Even tried and tested routines that I've been performing for years fail to hit the mark. So as I write, I'm having to see the show in my head, hearing my voice, and even occasionally saying it out loud. *NB This is not advised in coffee shops, libraries or any public environment!*

12th March, 2010 – Charlie Ross in "Carry On Camping"; CAPITOL, 8pm.

It's showtime!

Now here are some of the issues of putting on shows at "my level" of comedy. At the higher level, all the staging, technical stuff, setting up, is all done so the comedian just has to turn up and go on stage.

Not so for me and the likes of me.

I arrive at the venue early. I have a laptop to set up, I'm using a Powerpoint presentation with some clips on it, plus this has the music that I've prepared to play for when the audience is meandering in.

PLAYLIST:
We're Gonna Change The World – Matt Munro
Aquarela do Brasil - Ary Barrosso
The Trolley Song - Judy Garland

We're Off To See The Wizard – Judy Garland
The Banner Man – Blue Mink
Mamma Mia! – ABBA
Can't Taking My Eyes Off You – Andy Williams
The Court Of King Caractacus – Rolf Harris
Prince Charming – Adam and the Ants
My Coo Ca Choo – Alvin Stardust
Big Spender – Dame Shirley Bassey
Right Said Fred – Bernard Cribbins
Land Of Make Believe – Bucks Fizz
Such Trying Times – Marlene Dietrich
If I Love Ya Then I Need Ya – Eartha Kitt
Carry On Camping – Original Soundtrack

The powerpoint has to be checked. I could get anyone to work it, but you know I never quite trust anyone to do these, so I'll just do it myself.

Forty-eight distraught minutes later, we finally get the sound working, the projector is fine, there was a cabling issue and the laptop won't reach the stage! So I have to get one of the Go Button boys to do the Powerpoint for me, completely unrehearsed! I had this problem once before at a Doctor Who convention, the pc didn't work, the Powerpoint played up, and Tim didn't have a clue what was going on, but it worked because I made a joke or a "thing" of the whole débâcle, making it part of the show.

Worst comes to worst, this is, after all, a work in progress, so I can do the same again. I hurriedly write out some cues, myself and Graeme go through it, well it's not totally difficult. I can give him a cue from stage for each slide so what can go wrong?

Ahem!

The audience come in, sales are good. I hide away from view. The music is playing, we are, for all intents and purposes, good to go! I hear some faint titters from the crowd as the playlist moves from one silly camp song to another. There is even a little bit of a singalong to some, Prince Charming proved very popular (nostalgia is a powerful emotion)! I've cued up a Kenneth Williams-esque introduction, and I'm on stage.

When doing a full show, I and many other comics tend to effectively compère the first 5-10 minutes. This audience need time to get into the rhythm, so you set the tone and then get on with the show. This involves a bit of chat with the crowd, some friendly banter. Surprisingly, this is a very mixed audience. The front row consists of a group of teenagers, who sat there wide eyed in anticipation, with huge smiles on their faces – a plus for any comedian; they are ready and willing to laugh. But I can't help the thought going through my head, what on earth would bring them to a show called *Carry On Camping* is beyond me. Especially when I move onto the substance of the show: I mention Frankie Howerd and not one of them has a clue who he is! This actually isn't a problem, experience tells you not to let that kind of thing throw you, there is an opportunity to bounce the older members of the audience who are in sync with me, off against the younger. I do, however, feel a little nervous. Well it's a new show, new material, in fact the biggest proportion of new material I've put out there in one go since I began! So nerves are to be expected. So I hit the moment where my first slide has to be out up there. And to my horror and for no possible reason other than pure bad luck, the Powerpoint had jumped to the second last slide! So I have to labour thro getting it back to the start without, and this would have been the real disaster, leaving the stage. That disrupts the momentum, when that happens, ostensibly it's like starting again. So what do you do?

1. Make light of the situation
2. Suck it up and get it fixed – the Powerpoint constituted a large chunk of the show!

95

3. DON'T show any signs of panic – even though you are crumbling inside.

Now, of course poor Graeme got it in the neck. There has to be a fall guy and it can't be me, I have over an hour on stage left, the audience can't spend that thinking I'm an idiot, plus making light of it and to all intents and purposes, actually drawing attention TO it, means that when fixed it's done and dusted and the audience won't be thinking about it. If you try to ignore something like that then it becomes an elephant in the room, and you never quite get over it. And here is probably one of the most valuable pieces of advice.

EMBRACE FUCK-UPS!

They happen, they happen ALL the time. So don't pretend they don't happen, deal with them, talk about them, I promise all you budding comedians out there: the audience will generally love you for that! It shows humility and confidence in your abilities that you can handle anything. So laughing it off is always the best policy.

On this occasion, just that happened. In fact the audience warmed to me even more and the show went very well. Did all the new material hit the mark? No. Did it matter over the course of an hour and a half? Not really. Well not to the punters. Naturally I will go over every minute, analyse the reasons why some things worked and some didn't, tear the show apart and put it back together again, but that's my job, I need to do that. But the audience just need me to be generally funny for most of the time, they don't need to know how it works. I don't want to know how a plane flies, but I do want the pilot to know! Then he can worry about it.

So where next for *Carry On Camping?* I loved doing it, I'm very proud of it and I think it can get a lot better. The Fringe this year is out as there was a possibility of a bigger project coming off. So it looks like Fringe 2011. And the plus side is that I have my show, my blurb and the preparation way in advance of most people. A show in the bag over a year before Edinburgh is not usual, so I should be ahead of the game. Or will I just sit on it until I need to get it going again? Who knows, we're a fickle mob us comedians. A lot of us, and certainly I, could do with a bit more discipline. And discipline is where it's at. Although that doesn't always work for everyone. I see comedy around me, and I can wander around getting on with life for days and not see a thing, and then I can get a few routines out of a moment. Or a line will come up in conversation.

A Class of its Own

One of my favourite comedians of recent times is the US comic Doug Stanhope. He recently said on the subject of comedy classes, that anyone who teaches a comedy class is a parasite who exploits the stupidity of people who want to be stand-up comedians.

I think Stanhope was pretty much looking at how these classes go down Stateside, and I get the nature of his style is abrasive and provocative – that's what I love about him, he's the stand-up I could never have the balls to be. He uses examples of people running comedy courses who have little experience of actually working on the circuit, or charlatans who are talking up their career and knowledge. I'm with him there, but the same could be said of many courses, in any subject. And does a disservice to some of these comedy classes.

Up and down the country, many educational organizations have tapped into the concept of evening classes in stand up. And I teach one. Now in this case, and in an attempt to not be considered a parasite, I would contest that. To say that is to some extent a typical attitude amongst stand-ups today. It implies that a comedian is an entity all on his or her own, with no sense of working together with other comedians and no desire to craft your skills with feedback and discussion with others. This is one of the greatest assets of a class. Not everyone has the confidence to pursue the route that I did, heading straight for an open spot. The comfort zone of working in a group, under the guidance of someone with a bit of experience, is invaluable to some. As to exploiting stupidity or in some way taking advantage of those who want to be stand-ups... That is an arrogant and elitist statement that I have hated all my life. What about the kid in Physical Education classes who's the last to be picked for football or basketball? Does the fact that you may not be good at something preclude you from then trying it? Surely someone who may not be a naturally gifted comedian still has the fundamental right to give it a go? And the total contradiction of the statement is that there are many working and successful comedians who have chosen this path. I'm not suggesting for a second that they wouldn't have gained that success if they hadn't enrolled on a comedy class, but all would certainly agree that it helped. As Stu-Who? says, *"Comedy is an art-form. It's only pub entertainment if that's what you want to make it, and if that's what you want that's fine, but don't demean what others do in terms of the hard work they put into their craft. It's the purest art-form there is."*

There are many aspects of comedy performance that make it a craft. Maybe I cannot "teach" someone to be funny, but I can teach them many aspects of performance and the craft of this art-form that will help them to deliver what they write in the best possible way.

One of the first of its kind started at the University of Strathclyde in Glasgow under the auspices of Scottish stand up, and good friend of mine, Viv Gee.

"I was approached in 1998 about teaching the class. I did think first, is it possible to teach comedy? And then, who am I to teach others how to do it, I'd only been in stand-up for three years. So I was worried what people would think of me doing this."

Twelve years on and the class is still running, Viv is still gigging away so clearly something is working.

After a few years of doing stand-up myself there was one term that Viv couldn't take the class, and largely based on my teaching background as well as my stand-up experience, she asked me if I would stand in for her. Viv's class had already produced some formidable alumni including Des Mclean, Des Clarke, Reverend Obadiah Steppenwolf ...

So its reputation was a good one. I very much enjoyed the experience, and many years later on my return to Glasgow from London, a further education college in Glasgow asked me if I would be interested in doing such a class there. The class had run for one term but tragically, halfway through the class, the lecturer, by all accounts a lovely lady who had experience writing comedy for radio and had performed in the traditional club circuit, went on holiday and died.

The next term the class was started again with myself at the helm. Naturally, I was cautious about the trend set by people who took the class, but I bravely agreed. I have now been doing it for three years. There have been some successes – and when I say that, I mean there are former students who have gone on to perform, write and in a couple of cases, run comedy clubs. No major stars, so far, but that is pretty much what this book is about. Success is making money – ANY MONEY – out of comedy. If it's beer money, that's a success in my mind, it's still earning. After teaching a comedy workshop, Fred Macaulay says that the experience teaching comedy workshops to under-privileged kids in the Castlemilk area of Glasgow, "had the word WORTHY written all over it, but also in big letters was the word FEE."

It sounds ruthless. It's not. We all have to make a living, and Fred goes on to say that the kids had a fantastic time and for some a valuable one in terms of enhancing confidence and self-worth. Doug Stanhope, of course, would deny these kids that experience as they're probably too stupid to realize they are being taken advantage of.

However, I'm not going to talk about individuals here, I'm going to focus on the concept of teaching comedy. What exactly do we do in that classroom? In fact, it's the first thing most people say to me when I tell them I teach an evening class in stand-up comedy.

"How can you teach people to be funny?"

If I were to place my hand on my heart, and as I've already implied, I'm not entirely sure you can. Three years, nine terms of classes in, I'm still not sure. Does that make me a con artist? A parasite? Well ok, I'll try to justify the fee that I take for the class.

I have already talked about "funny bones". There are those who have it, and those who don't. We all know who we're talking about. A mate you may have who can recount a story or a joke in the pub with aplomb and confidence. Those with the patter to chat people up, use humour to diffuse tricky situations, you know who I mean.

Now here is the paradox. Those guys with funny bones often make passable comedians. Some don't. Conversely, someone who has never made anyone laugh in the pub in their life, can also stand on stage and get away with being a comedian. Personally, I'm always more interested in the naturally funny. The best example is Billy Connolly. You only have to look at Connolly to know that he has always had that innate ability to not only make people laugh, but to look at the world from a different angle. I've sat in many a green room with comedians, some very successful, who are the most terminally dull people off stage I've ever met. And you only have to spend five minutes with someone to spot that they have simply never made their mates in the pub laugh spontaneously. EVER. For that ability is a mixture of natural personality, confidence, wit, charm and viewpoint. However, it IS possible to construct that for a stage performance. And I suppose that's fair enough, if you're on stage, making the audience laugh, then you're earning your wages. For those people, confidence is the predominant factor. There is a saying, that in any form of public address, it's 20% what you say, and 80% how you say it. It's for that reason that politicians continually get away with misleading voters. It's presence and aura. And some have it. The question is, are they faking it?

To an extent, yes they are. And to me, this creates a separation. The naturally funny comedian is fluid, organic, the same routine can be changed, tweaked, moved around in the moment, adjusted to suit, and in the case of the best in the business, ditched completely because something better has just come into their head. The comedian who isn't naturally funny is pulling off a performance that has none of that fluidity. It is structured, organized, with every "i" dotted and every "t" crossed. It is a comedy "performance," and therein lies the difference. Now, remember, this is personal, a preference, I'm not saying what those guys are doing is bad, it's just a different approach. But they will always be a certain type of performer, and of course, that has restrictions. These are the comedians that struggle when nights don't go exactly to plan. Comedy audiences have a habit of being unpredictable. On those nights, the comedian with "funny bones" can often use this natural wit to get out of a tricky situation, or deviate from the routine to get an audience on track.

Back to the point of the chapter. Can you teach someone to be funny? My honest answer? No. Can you develop skills that can make someone come across as funny on a stage? Yes, of course.

There tend to be certain categories of people who come to the comedy class.

1. The funny ones who know it

2. The non-funny ones who know it

3. The funny ones who don't know it

4. The non-funny ones who think they're funny

5. Any of the above who regardless of whether they are 1-4, just keep trying to be funny all the live long day!

Here, I am loath to give away too much of what I do in class, because I don't want to do myself out of a job, but most of the stuff is interactive and requires less talking from me, and more from them.

I made a conscious decision early on that the class would not be a theory one. There are plenty of books, and I'm sure Open University courses, that teach the theory of how comedy works, what a joke is, what kinds of jokes there are, and I do know a lot of that. But this is a performance course, it is ten weeks in duration with a performance in front of a live audience on week nine – week ten is the feedback and reflection week – not a lot of time. So I don't want to get bogged down in talking about comedy.

Now some students come with ideas for routines already, some have written material but just want to mix with like-minded people before trying it out on stage. This is one big advantage to starting out in comedy. It's a lonely game, even for open spots. There isn't the same camaraderie you get in a drama performance, every act on the bill is there to score their own penalty, you are pretty much on your own. So it is appealing to spend ten weeks in the company of others who are generally at the same stage and are like-minded. I did it on my own, but I do find the idea of starting this way quite appealing. Of course when you start out you very quickly make friends but as far as writing material and developing, and also getting feedback, there is no "workshop" mentality. Comedians, no matter what stage in their career, don't tend to meet up to discuss the nuances of their own performances. There is no continuing professional development. Promoters will either book you again, or they won't, that is generally the feedback. So to spend some time with other people in that workshop environment isn't too bad an idea.

What is the first stage? Well, the best one is to find out why they are there. And surprisingly, the reasons are wide and varied.

Top of the obvious pile is to be a professional stand-up comedian. The next is to be famous (and that's a distinction I've discussed elsewhere). Another is to gain confidence in public speaking, or to help with giving presentations at work. For others it's a life experience thing, and of course one of the major reason to do an evening class in the first place – just to get out of the house!

So where do I begin?

The first major starting point is to tell a story. And there is only one condition here, it has to be a true story. It doesn't even have to be funny, just true. The reason for this is, one of the biggest problems facing you in the early days, and certainly in your first gig, is the overwhelming and crippling nerves. One of the first things that nerves do is blank your mind, and make you forget. If your routine is based on a true story, then at least you won't forget the story, you won't be standing there in dead air.

Once the story is told, then we look for chances to "gag it up." Now some people just get it, they spot the beat in any story or even joke, where there are opportunities for jokes. And a lot of "story-telling" comedians do just that. Tell a story that is embellished, looking for any opportunity to look for a joke.

Ok, so here is an example.

So I got on the tube the other day. It was jam-packed, really busy. I squeezed into the carriage. The doors were about to close, when someone ran onto the platform convinced he could make it. He leapt towards the train and just about managed to squeeze onto the train but his rucksack got caught between the doors. He panicked and pulled the rucksack through the now closed doors, but in the process a pile of papers fell out, some on the platform, lost forever as the doors were now closed, and others scattered on the carriage floor, which were impossible to pick up as it was so busy. The guy stood there, a little embarrassed, as I and other passengers exchanged wry smiles.

That's a true story, it happened to me on the London tube last year. It's only slightly amusing at best. In fact this is now one of my best and most consistently bankable routines. How come?

Well, I'm not going to write out the routine. For a start, some if it is visual, and second, as with all stand-up comedy, works best in performance.

(Try it, pick your favourite comedy routine by your absolute favourite comedian. Write it out verbatim and then read it back. Then give it to someone who hasn't seen the routine to read. You'll be astonished at how unfunny it reads, you will giggle a few times because you've seen it, the other person may not even laugh at all!)

But I will show you how I came to develop this moderately amusing story into a routine I am proud of.

First, does the story work in retelling? Well yes because it's a common or shared experience. A lot of the audience will have been on a busy train at some point, some even on the London Underground, and a lot will certainly have either seen one of these idiots who think they possess the power to pass through solid objects as the doors close, or may even BE one of them. So it works on that level. Now let's look at the story again, but I'll break it down. At this stage, I'm looking for the jokes, where you can "gag it up". So I've put in some notes.

So I got on the tube the other day. **Joke about London? The tube?** *It was jam-packed, really busy.* **Jam-packed like...? Joke there!** *I squeezed in to the carriage.* **Closeness, rubbing up against others?** *The doors were about to close, when someone ran onto the platform convinced he could make it.* **Definite joke about idiots who do this!** *He leapt towards the train and just about managed to squeeze onto the train but his rucksack got caught between the doors.*

JOKE! *He panicked and pulled the rucksack through the now closed doors, but in the process a pile of papers fell out, some on the platform,* **Could the whole rucksack become separated by the arm straps?** *lost forever as the doors were now closed, and others scattered on the carriage floor, which were impossible to pick up as it was so busy. The guy stood there, a little embarrassed, as I and other passengers exchanged wry smiles.* **NEEDS A PUNCHLINE!**

Now, that's very basic and gives very little away about what the routine does. But for those of you who are interested, the routine is on YouTube, and the link is on my website. Don't say I'm not good to you!

Hopefully you will see how the routine gets built. I believe for a lot of those who come on the course, this is a good starting point. It helps to see how a joke works, what kinds of jokes come naturally to the story and gets them thinking of the rhythm inherent in building a routine. Of course, not all of the class want to do that style of comedy. Some want to be joke tellers, in the style of Jimmy Carr, or surrealists like Ross Noble, and that's fine. I certainly don't insist they follow my recommendation, but most do, and if you don't well all I can say is the jokes should be good, and you better have a good memory. And if you're doing surreal comedy you should be prepared to accept that a percentage of the audience won't buy into it, that comes with the territory. A high percentage of comedy-goers is tuned in to the story telling style. So as a starting point, and just to get the beginner going, it's what I suggest. Once those first few experiences have passed, then that style may change, but I believe it is the best for this situation.

So once they have decided on the story or potential routine, where do they go from there? We start to gag it up, perform it, develop it, workshop it, and hopefully make the best routine we can. And it's a collective process, which often, stand-up comedy writing isn't. But there are quite a few other skills that can be developed. I've already said I don't believe I can MAKE someone funny, but I can provide them with the tools to give them the best chance of being funny.

There are many tricks, techniques of the trade, but there is one major tool. The microphone. The microphone gives the comedian his power, it is the transmission unit for the voice and the medium through which the comic gets his material out there. Now some comedians get away without it, Ian Cognito is a master of it and you can read all about him later. But to almost all of us, the microphone is equivalent to Harry Potter's magic wand, or Jimmy Page's guitar; it is our conduit to the audience. Using a microphone to it's maximum potential is an art in itself and when you see it done at its best it can be extremely effective. And the hand held is the best for this, a radio mic certainly frees up your whole body but the hand held mic allows you to add effects to your voice, emphasizing tone and volume when required, and adds a great deal of colour to the routine.

There is also so much to teach about stance, delivery, voice, timing. Although, that's not to be said that a lot of those things aren't natural. It is impossible to account for natural timing, presence and that much used word, gravitas. It is the easiest thing in the world to spot when someone has this, they step in front of an audience, any audience, and there is a presence. It's kind of like being able to spot a good footballer, you can tell almost immediately by the way they address the ball, the posture over the ball and the way they move around the pitch with grace and poise. These are all things that a natural performer has. And those cannot be taught. They can however be enhanced, nurtured. Anyone in any field of performance can be given guidelines on how to improve what they already have, but can one teach these? Can you teach someone to be naturally funny? I honestly don't think so. That's not to say that

107

someone can't be guided towards "being funny" on stage. There is a difference.

It is important to say that as a comic, you're always learning. No comedian is the finished article. And I mean nobody. Because you're constantly searching for a better way to do what you do, or hunting down that style or voice that will elevate you onto another level. And of course, until you can perform in any gig, to any audience, at any time, and be guaranteed that you will always do well, which almost no comedian can do – recently Billy Connolly received a lukewarm response at a gig in Glasgow, which would seem to be almost a criminal offence – so until you can do that, then the comic is always learning.

Comedians are often very guilty of both giving and receiving! Ooh missus, but I mean feedback. We don't discuss our sets with other comics unless they are very close friends, and you rarely work with your best friends. I'm almost never on the same bill as Scott Agnew, probably my best mate in comedy, as we're both gay and to have two gay acts on the same bill is against a law that I think is in Leviticus somewhere, so we rarely get to see each other. And we absolutely should do this, we should constantly teach each other. There are tricks we all have and that should be shared if it's going to make someone's set better. Stu-Who? recalls the value of the early days of the Funny Farm. This was a group of comedians that included Stu, Fred Macaulay, Bruce Morton and Parrott, all Scottish acts, which started as an evening of comedy in Blackfriars in Glasgow and eventually made it to television when commissioned by Scottish Television in 1993. Stu says, *"It was great to do, and helped us all as individual stand-ups."*

Have I seen any of that natural talent in my classes so far? Definitely. But like anything, once they are sent on their way, there are so many factors that may lead to them becoming a comedian that are random, and down to honest hard work. But the class can be a useful starting point, if only to meet others who have the same interest, and like most evening classes, to get the hell out of the house!

The Spin Offs

A career in comedy can just be about the live stage work, but of course, as a performer, there is always a chance that this leads to other kinds of work. This other work can be interesting, sometimes challenging, a little extra money, and often exposure.

The first off-shoot I had was to work in radio. BBC Radio Scotland often uses local talent to guest spot on various shows. My very first appearance was on a show called Lafferty Out Loud. The show was hosted by a Glasgow-based lawyer, Austin Lafferty, who had made his media reputation on Scottish Television news doing the legal expert spot. The show itself was a late night chat show about various topics that had cropped up in the news that week. Now these shows are never hard-hitting, the idea being to take the lighter news items and make fun of them and expand the discussion accordingly. The show was always fun to do, and could at times be unpredictable. On one occasion there was an enormous fit of pique when a young dancer was invited onto the show as ballet was one of the topics. Now this was recorded on a Friday night at 11pm, so it's easy to understand that this girl, nervous about making an appearance on national radio (I say national from a Scottish perspective of course), had made a stop off at one of the many public houses on Byres Road as she walked up to the BBC studios which were then housed in Queen Margaret Drive. She should maybe have stopped after just the one, because she was, how can I put this politely, pissed as a fart, when she appeared. In the studio there were frequently fits of giggles and swear to god, I was able to talk about the ballet with a greater degree of expertise than she was. It all came to a peak when she underlined a "point" she was making with a redoubtable shriek of "FUCK!" I just laughed but remember this is Radio Scotland, it's twee, it's late night knitting, it's the Sunday Post, it's... you get the idea. This was akin to supporting Al Qaeda on the national news, or putting on twitter that Stephen Fry's a cunt (he's so not by the way!). I thought the producer was going to pass out, and Austin did his level best to float somewhere between consummate professional and teenage boy as he suppressed the giggles.

The promotion from Lafferty Out Loud was to the Fred Macaulay Show. Fred, one of the UK's finest stand-up comedians, has his own morning show on Radio Scotland. A very similar flavour to Austin's show, a light-hearted look at news stories with special guests. These could be anyone from A-list celebs who want to plug something to working comedians like myself or experts in a certain field. But the tone is always light. Nobody says "fuck" on Fred's show, and if you did, you would certainly never be asked back. I've always enjoyed doing the Macaulay show and continue to do so, in fact I am preparing to go on it next week to do a feature called "Five Things." Usually this feature is to take five headlines of the week and chat about the ones that most intrigue the guest. Next week's is different, it's 80's day on the channel and the feature is to focus on five stories from the 80's. Now there are of course obvious ones, Charles and Diana getting married, Live-Aid, the Berlin Wall coming down, and I may mention these but I'll also research to try and prompt some memories and come up with some more obscure stories.

I've spoken at length about my work in the world of Doctor Who conventioning, but that work led to my appearances in audio Doctor Who adventures for a company called Big Finish. In the 90's when the Time Lord was not as hip as he is today, Big Finish obtained a licence to do audio stories featuring some of the actors who played the Doctor and his companions in the classic series.

111

Sadly, the legendary Tom Baker is so far the only surviving Doctor from the original series who hasn't made an appearance with Big Finish, but hope springs eternal. They are very persuasive and passionate, so I'm sure they will tempt him into one at some point.

After doing a cabaret at a convention in Swansea called Regenerations, two lovely actors who at that point were audio companions to Paul McGann's Doctor, India Fisher and Conrad Westmass, dragged me to meet Gary Russell who was one of the founder members of Big Finish, and writer/director on the stories. India and Conrad, who had enjoyed my show, were encouraging Gary to get me into a Big Finish story. Well after a few drinks and in the euphoria of a great event, this is often just chit chat and there is a feeling of going through the motions. Details were exchanged and you never really expect anything to come of it. However, true to his word, within two weeks, Gary emailed me to offer me the part of a villain in a story with Paul McGann, India and Conrad. To say I was delighted is putting it mildly. And I am forever indebted to Gary for offering me that opportunity, as that story, *Memory Lane*, led to other Big Finish work and I have to date appeared in the following:

Memory Lane with Paul McGann,
Gallifrey with Louise Jameson, Lalla Ward and John Leeson,
City of Spires with Colin Baker and Frazer Hines,
Legend of the Cybermen with Colin Baker, Frazer Hines and Wendy Padbury.

"Gallifrey" is a spin-off from the Doctor Who range, a tale of political intrigue on the Time Lords' home world. Louise Jameson played Leela opposite Tom Baker in the 70's and in an illustrious career, went on to star in Tenko, Bergerac and Eastenders. It was at the recording of Gallifrey that I first met Louise and she has gone on to become a wonderful friend and amazing support in my career. The same can be said for many people I worked with on Big Finish work, Colin Baker is a friend and an inspiration. Frazer Hines is also a very good mate, we share a similar sense of humour. It's always a pleasure to catch up with him and all my new friends from the world of Doctor Who.

It astounds me that I, as a lifelong fan of this wonderful show, have not only met many of my heroes, but have worked with them and couldn't in my wildest dreams have anticipated that I would become a friend to them. Astonishing.

So when Nicholas Briggs, another co-founder of Big Finish and now best known for brilliantly doing the voices of the Daleks and Cybermen in the new TV series of "Who," asked me to play Rob Roy in two stories, one of which with the Cybermen, you can only imagine my reaction.

Nick directed both stories and was brilliant to work with. He does the Cyberman voice there and then, using a ring modulator to change his voice accordingly. As a fan, that in itself was brilliant, but I went into a booth to record a scene, now knowing that Nick had been doing a scene as a Cyberman in that booth just before me. They had left the ring modulator on and when I spoke into it, my voice had been converted to cyberness! In an instant I was 10 years old and having fun talking in the metallic drone of these monsters I had watched as a small child and had been terrified of. Nick himself, I still think, connects with the child that we all have in ourselves when doing it, and it's probably because of that shared excitement that I heard him say from the booth, "Switch it to number 9 and give him a Dalek." Well. That was amazing! It's scary how power hungry and manic you get when you sound like a Dalek! I loved it. Thanks Nick!

And thanks to Gary Russell as well, without whom... etc. Gary left Big Finish a few years ago and went to work in Cardiff on the TV show itself, fulfilling another life-long dream, culminating in getting to be script editor on the two part story *"The End of Time"* which brought the reign of David Tennant as the Doctor to an end. That was fantastic for Gary, and well deserved.

The likes of myself, Nick and Gary have all had the honour of doing a paid job that involves the TV show that we have loved for the largest part of our lives. It certainly proves the old adage that if you find a job you love, you'll never work a day in your life!

Another job that came up as a result of a gig turned out to be one of the most enjoyable things I've ever done, and cemented my desire to make movies.

I was approached after a gig in Jongleurs Glasgow by a film director who was making a short film. Gary Thomas is a London-based film-maker who has made a few short films focussing on diversity. He said he had written the part of a gay PE teacher! Well, it's fair to say that I was probably the only actor in the country who filled those criteria. It was my first opportunity to act in front of the camera, so of course I jumped at it.

Over three days in Buckinghamshire, I spent a fabulous time with some wonderful people and ended up making some great friends and learning an awful lot about the filming process. I was playing one of the two main parts, the other being a fine young actor called Graeme Dalling. I had helped Gary in the audition process, which basically involved kissing handsome actors for an afternoon, what a drag that was! And curiously, of the six actors we looked at, Graeme stood out but I'm pretty sure he was the only straight one. He had a quality, a look, just something that worked. In fact, the process made me feel a lot better about the auditioning process.

Usually after an audition, regardless of how you felt it went, you don't get any feedback. You either get the part or you don't.

So as you can imagine, in the paranoid mind of your average actor/entertainer, your default position is:

I WAS SHITE!

And there are many auditions I've left feeling good, and confident that I couldn't have done any better. But that kind of logic doesn't really apply here. For a start, you have no frame of reference, no idea what a director is looking for, and certainly not what others have done. It is a very cold process, and a long wait to see if there is a call from your agent to tell you they want to see you again or, even better, you have the part!

My attitude changed somewhat after this process. First I was amazed at the highly qualified and experienced young actors who were keen to be involved. This was a *very* low budget film. And only a few days' work, but it showed me that actors, and I mean every actor, wants to work. Regardless of what you've done, or about to do, they all want to keep at it. Like building a portfolio.

We looked at six actors, and here is the case in point. One of them was so not right for the part. But any of the other five could have done the part no problem. Some just looked maybe slightly too young, another slightly too old, which of course they can do nothing about. No amount of talent can make up for what you're bringing to a part physically. And it was down to two. Graeme and another actor whose name I sadly cannot remember. But they were both great. I seem to recall thinking that the other lad was a touch too posh for the part, but that's not a major issue. However, in one tiny moment, Graeme gave me a look, a glance, I mean almost nothing. But that got him the part. I thought so, Gary agreed and there you were, he was cast. Now my point of course is that the others will leave thinking they've done well and will then torture themselves as to what they did wrong. Thing is, for the most part, they did nothing wrong. The margin of error was so tiny. You want to call them and let them know that they were fine, great even, and to encourage them that in this crazy world, it can come down to almost anything.

Other work that has come my way, underlines this. I have been to many castings for adverts. Now commercials can be soul destroying but they are often good money and can be good exposure. But even more so, these castings are based entirely on a look, a sound, basically, they are cosmetic. No amount of experience on stage, or even ten years at the Royal Shakespeare Company will make any difference. This is clear from the second you walk in the door. Immediately, there is a look on the faces of those auditioning you. Every fibre in your being is tempted to just turn around and walk out, but you dance the dance, you never know, something else might come up that you may be right for.

Curiously, I've been cast in two commercials. One was an ident for Sky Sports. Idents are the brief mini-ads that you get just before a programme, or to promote something. Usually no more than fifteen seconds. I went to a casting for one which simply involved watching a football match with some mates in the pub and cheering as a goal is scored. At the time I was based in Glasgow, but happened to be in London at the time of the casting, handy! Went along, went ok, then nothing, no call for over a week. That's that then. About three months later, I got a call from my agent saying they wanted me to do one. Excellent. Filming was in London, they flew me down, and I went along to the pub that was being used, and as is always the case here, it was very early in the morning.

The ident was for Sky Bet, which Sky Sports were promoting, the premise being that a viewer could place a bet on just about anything in the game or sport they were watching. Now naturally I assumed they had spotted my athleticism at the audition, my years of experience as a PE teacher were about to pay off. I turned up and walked in only to be told I was playing a DARTS PLAYER! They handed me this typical bawdy darts shirt and told me to get practising. One of the best things about a film shoot is the catering, this one had a big double-decker bus and a great choice of grub. Only, on this occasion the catering bus was the highlight. Filming is pretty dull at the best of times. But waiting around to see which camera angle would be best to show the darts board was not my idea of fun. In the end, when the ad went out, all you saw was me briefly cheering on a shot in a darts match. And even then, if you didn't have a wide-screen TV, all you saw was my fist! Weird thing is, they flew me down from Glasgow, put me up in a hotel, paid me my fee, just to shake my fist in the air at a darts shot. Are you seriously telling me that not one actor in London could have done that? As I said, it's a look, nothing to do with talent. But as I said, the food was great.

At least in that ad you saw something of me, in the other commercial I made, I played an advisor in a Job Centre to promote a new benefits scheme. Yet again, it's a dull day. They kitted me out in a shirt, tie and trousers. You wouldn't believe the time that it took to decide whether a Job Centre advisor would wear a blue or a white shirt. I'm pretty sure even actual Job Centre advisors don't put anything like that level of effort into what they wear. In my experience, most put no effort in, but that just may be the Job Centres I've experienced.

This was filmed in an actual Job Centre in the west end of Glasgow, namely Partick. At 5pm, all the job seekers and staff were bundled out of the building and a group of bohemian-looking extras were trailed in. Can I say, none of these "supporting artists," as they're called now, looked anything like the actual people who had been in half an hour earlier!

As usual, you're dressed, made up, then asked to sit about for four hours mostly being ignored. I had one, yes *one* line. The line was, "There's no pressure, and we'll even make sure you won't lose any of your benefits!"

117

Naturally, when I was finally front and centre I kept saying: "There's no pressure, and we'll even make sure you *lose* all your benefits!"

The director kept asking me to speak more quietly, apparently I was projecting too much, darling.

When the ad was finally on TV, I saw the first bit of it, got excited thinking, *this is it*, waited with baited breath for my little bit at the end of the ad, and then...... NOTHING. They cut me out! And to this day, I have no idea why! Was the ad too long? Did I not, as it turned out, look right? Was my performance shit? Who knows, and I'll never know. All I know is that the cheque cleared and I got some credit cards paid down. One thing I will say, is that I was cast because I looked friendly and had a nice smile, and yet the person who played the other Job Centre advisor played as a right torn-face cow with no personable qualities at all! So in my mind, the government, who commissioned the ad, didn't want anyone thinking that Job Centre staff were even remotely nice. Wouldn't want that, would we? As I said, that's just in my head. There are many other bits and pieces you can pick up from gigging on the circuit, other things I've done, scripts and plays I've written for example kind of came separately, but there is no doubt that being a stand-up can lead to many other avenues being explored.

Final Thoughts

I have no idea whether any of this will be useful to you if you want to go into the world of comedy. All I can say with confidence is that that's the way I did it. And remember, I made a *lot* of mistakes on the way. But I wouldn't have my life or career any other way. Would I like more exposure, more success? Sure. Actually, what I would like is simply to be working all the time, and maybe to have a degree of choice over the gigs I take. And to be fair, that's exactly what every comedian I've chatted to for this book has agreed on. That success on any level to a comedian means being in constant work. The occasional weekend off aside, we all want to be thinking on a Wednesday night, "Right, where am I this weekend? What have I got to prepare?" That is really what we all really desire.

On this road I have met some amazing people, and would actually say I have found some of my best and hopefully life-long friends. I don't know where I would have been in the last few years without Scott Agnew. I swear to God I'd be in the tall grass. Actually I'd probably have given up. You see, this is a very emotional game. On a regular basis, you are baring your soul on stage and asking people to laugh at it. That takes its toll on you as a person. It's no wonder that many comedians are highly strung, or mentally challenged in one way or another. The depressive state of the comic is well documented. *The tears of a clown,* etc. And that's where I owe so much to my friends in the business. And also to friends who aren't! In the early days, we all rely so much on the goodwill of those nearest and dearest to us. They make sacrifices too. Whether it's a partner who has to lose you to this weird world from one weekend to the next, or the mates that you are constantly badgering to come along to gigs for moral or financial support. It is a struggle. But then life is generally a struggle, and I cannot begin to say how wonderful a reward the comedian gets for that struggle when he stands on stage and feels that laughter coming back at him. As I said way back at the start of this book, that feeling of exhilaration, the rush, the sheer energy of feeling the laughter of an audience storming at you like a tidal wave onto the stage. There are very few jobs that offer you that feeling. And after you've felt that once, it never goes away, and it's crazily addictive. It's what makes up for the times when the tidal wave coming back to you is one of silence, or worse, indifference.

As I write these last notes on this book, Chris Rea's song "The Road to Hell" has come on the radio. Is that a sign? When we embark on the well-travelled road of the stand up comedian, is that a normal road we are setting out on, or is it a Yellow Brick Road? It can be both, it just really depends on many factors. But most importantly it depends on three things: hard work, discipline, and how funny your bones are.

Some More Stuff

To round off this book, on the following pages are some articles I've written for various publications over the years. Are they padding? Oh you cynical sod you, the simple answer to that is yes. But I think they're worthy of getting a wider audience. All of them were written for various gay publications, including Scotsgay magazine, whose then editor, Martin Walker should be cited as being an incredible support and help in my career both in comedy and in writing. Hope you enjoy them!

Keep Your Hands to Yourself
ScotsGay Magazine, April 2008

So I'm on Glasgow's excuse for an underground. The transport system that sits somewhere between the London Docklands Railway and the monorail at Disneyland. The tiny orange carriage is hurtling through the tunnel system, this is not the Victoria or Piccadilly line, just a bloody circle that goes round and round, stopping every 50 seconds to toss off a few people. Which actually sounds a bit like my love life! So the carriage is quite busy. Everyone is doing that very British thing of expending 100 calories a minute trying to not engage anyone else in visual contact, or any other kind of contact. For a gay man, this underground is very different to London, where you only have to catch another guy's eyes for anything over 10 seconds to be shagging him in his flat within 30 minutes. Not here in this sexless orange tube of doom, there is no chance of anything happening.

However. Directly across from me is a young man. He has messy hair, some piercings in his, well I think every available place you can get one, and a few that shouldn't be! Every inch of skin on his arms is covered in tattoos and they are also creeping up like poison ivy onto his neck, sliding eerily towards his face as if about to engulf his entire being. His fingernails are painted black, naturally, as if Freddie Mercury hadn't buried that trend in 1974! And the extremely thin legs have the obligatory extra tight black jeans as if to emphasise his skinniness. Oh the pride of having absolutely no leg muscles. How do those legs manage to support him for goodness sake? Beside him, no, locked onto him like the space shuttle onto the international space station is the female version of, well, him!

Seriously, give him fake boobs and an attitude and he would be her! They are intently engaged in each other. Pecking and prodding every possible space they can. And then it happens. The peck on the lips is held, the mouths open, and the tongue massage begins. No, no, no, no, NO! The only thing I can think of is where I can get a bucket of ice cold water and drench the pair in it. Because this is the one aspect of social behaviour I feel most uncomfortable with, public displays of affection. PDA's for the more technically minded!

So, there they are. Going at it hammer and tongs. The atmosphere in the train is decidedly cagey. I mean what is it? Don't they get to do that anywhere else? Does either of them think the other is going to run away with the first available person if they don't give each other maximum attention? Or is their love for each other just so deep, a love that only they know, where they look into each others eyes, see their souls and confront each other in a moment of human honesty? Nah, it's bullshit, they're just showing off.

I'm sensitive to it, you see. Doubly sensitive in fact. Firstly, if I did that with a bloke all hell would break loose. Well maybe not, it is Britain after all, most people would just feel even more uncomfortable. But there is the risk of being on the receiving end of violent or verbal abuse by idiots who thought Brian Souter and Adolf Hitler should get Humanitarian honours! And secondly, being single, I naturally don't want anyone else to be happy in a relationship. Yes, yes, I'm bitter. And at this particular juncture in my life, a little proud of it.

So what is it with PDA's? Is it smugness, when two people find each other, do they want to share it with the whole world? Truth be told, even when in a relationship it's not something I like to indulge in. I believe that some things are for private time, and if you share those quieter moments with all and sundry, it somehow belittles those special moments. In company it's just plain rude and yes, there is an element of showing off. Or covering up cracks. The last thing that any couple wants to do is show any chinks in the armour of its perfect existence. So, I just can't leave you alone, or someone might spot that we actually don't want to be together anymore!

I see them all the time on the streets of any city. The GAP couple, dressed immaculately from head to toe in designer labels, walking along the road with one hand in each others back pocket and the other holding hands in front. Don't they know that one of the advantages of being human is that if you fall, your hands are there to protect you? How much do I want to trip up the fuckers and see their smug faces crash onto the cold, cracked pavement? Too much? Oh well, we can all have our fantasies. And when you get in their way, they are not for budging. No I have to negotiate my way all the way around them, because anyone who deigns to be single must move out of the way for the smug bastards.

The gay scene doesn't get any better. Now, for the purposes of this article, I'm not including sex in toilets or parks as PDA's. That's just not fair. Hypocrite? Me? I'm a single gay man in a world that says I should have to pay double the price for food because its all designed for two, throw most of it out because I can't eat all of it before it goes off and don't expect to get asked to dinner parties anymore, because the single person just reminds the couples of how depressed they were before they met! Yes, I'm a hypocrite, I'm allowed my faults. But yes, on the scene the PDA's are in full flow. Now I don't always begrudge this. After all, it is the one public place where gay men and women can show affection for each other without fear of attack. And in the early throes of passion, it is understandable that one may want to indulge in a little tonsil hockey with the significant other. But let's do it for the right reasons. If it's to show off, then try and remember what it was like to be single. If it's to paper over the cracks, then talk to your partner, it will

125

be more productive. If it's because you just don't know what to do with your hands, then take an evening class. I hear macramé is making a comeback!

Taking the X Out Of Christmas
ScotsGay Magazine, December 2008

Are you hanging up the stocking on the wall? Snow is falling, everywhere (well, most parts of the Arctic circle maybe, and parts of the Alps, not quite everywhere!). Are your chestnuts roasting on an open fire? Yes, it's that time of year again. The time when Noddy Holder is the happiest man in the music business, the time we USED to care what was going to be number one – but now no-one gives a shit – and the one time in the year when I actually listen to a Mariah Carey song through choice! (It really *is* a great song, but doesn't mean I don't still think she's a cunt!)

I have to admit it, I am a Christmas freak. I love it. I love the decorations, I love the songs, I love the food, I REALLY love the drink. It's great, I buy into it all. I watch It's A Wonderful Life, The Sound of Music and The Wizard of Oz with the kind of dedication a heroin addict seeking out his next fix. I make mulled wine, heat up the mince pies, roast chestnuts – yes we all like mince and nuts at Chrimble, don't we?
WARNING- this article may contain nuts, mince and any other camp innuendo the writer can manage!

There are things I don't like. I can't stand inappropriate Christmas. Selection Boxes on our supermarket shelves in August? What's that all about? The marketing frenzy is nuts, and totally out of hand. They'll be draping tinsel on the sun tan lotion in Boots next! "FREE SET OF CHRISTMAS CARDS WITH EVERY TWO EASTER EGGS!"

I hate Xmas! NO, not Christmas, XMAS! That fucker of a lazy abbreviation. "Let's replace the word Christ with a cross of some kind, because firstly it makes the word shorter, cos writing the whole thing is just a hassle, and second, it's a sort of respect, innit?" No, it's bloody not! I'm no religious man, but the guy roamed about Palestine 2,000 years ago, said a few cool things and everyone in the Christian world STILL talks about him and celebrates his birthday every year. Plus, he managed to pick up twelve boys and a prostitute while he was at it. The man deserves a little credit, for crying out loud!

I really hate people who don't like Christmas. Like those with kids, the people for whom it should be a wonderful thing, a magical time. "You don't understand," they say, "You don't have kids, you don't know how hard it is to cope with all the stuff they want." Well, here's a thought. TEACH THEM SOME VALUES!

You're the one in charge, don't give in just cause it's easier to buy an X-box than to actually talk to your children and give them a little understanding of compassion and selflessness. Also, don't you hate it when some hetties act as if their children were foisted upon them? You know, as if they were left on the doorstep one day and they were forced to raise them. It's not *my* fault *you* can't enjoy a child-free Christmas!

So there you go. Addicted to festivity. Which is strange considering how many Christmas Days have been so downright miserable.

Christmas is a strange time for gays and lesbians. Often detached from family through geography, estrangement or choice! Partners – despite all the recent civil liberty shenanigans – aren't quite embraced as the loving son- or daughter-in-law. So often, gay couples are wrenched apart at Christmas, enduring family arguments, disappointing presents and the inevitable questions from the old aunties who haven't spotted the clues – "When are you going to meet a nice girl and get married?"

Often, gay men and women choose to spend Christmas with their new family, friends who are in a similar situation.

Regardless of how you spend your Christmas and to whatever extent it's a camp one, this surely is the time of year for tolerance and understanding. Try to have Christmas on your terms, don't buy expensive presents if you can't afford it, don't suffer the shops on a Saturday afternoon, don't go to the office party if you really can't bear it. No-one will think the worse of you for it, and you'll probably enjoy the festive season all the more for it!

So what will make the ultimate gay Christmas then?

Take in a camp festive concert, always good to give the lungs a work out and do all the actions to The Twelve Days Of Christmas, we always do it far better than the straights anyway!

If you go to a work night out, don't lie and say you're heading off early cos you're tired, proudly announce that you are in fact going to a gay bar with the hope of some seasonal sex. That'll crowd the water cooler the next day!

Get a Christmas playlist on your MP3 player. It helps raise the festive spirit when you're wandering around the shops or running on the treadmill.

Go skating! Camp as tits, and a good excuse to dig out the ear muffs.

Watch Doctor Who on Christmas Day. Best show on telly, where it should be, prime time at Christmas!

Well, I'm going off to kick back with some hot nuts and a glass of mulled wine and watch crap telly wearing nothing but a Santa hat! Now that's Christmas, I might even have Mariah blaring in the background. And why not, Christmas only comes once a year!

NOTE:
Bizarrely, when this article was published, the editor didn't pick up on the point that I was making about the spelling of Christmas versus Xmas and published them all with the former spelling, rendering the

point of the article redundant! So you are reading this in its proper form for the first time ever..... editors, eh? Always know best!

The following two articles cover a similar theme, and indeed some points are repeated. But it's worth putting in as it extends some thoughts and ideas. Tell you what, read them on different days!

From BASE Magazine, July 2008

Article from The Sun, July 15th 2019:

The stars were out in numbers today for the "wedding" of Harry Potter star Daniel Radcliffe to his long term boyfriend, Jamie Bell. The couple, who have been dating for six years, finally tied the knot at a registry office in west London. Radcliffe, 30, said he was over the moon.

"Jamie is the best guy ever, I'm so lucky".

The Billy Elliott star Bell, 33, looked delighted as they posed for photographs. They were whisked off to their honeymoon in the south of France where we're sure Harry Potter will work some magic with his wand!

Among the high profile guests were Toby Maguire, Stephen Fry, Sir Ian McKellen and Tom Cruise, accompanied by his 12th wife, Abigail Breslin. They were all eclipsed as the day was given the Royal seal of approval as Prince William arrived with his girlfriend, Maria-Antonia Vicenza. Unperturbed by recent reports that Miss Vicenza was actually born George Duckworth in Manchester, the couple insisted the wedding in August would go ahead.

Also there was movie heart-throb and 5 times Oscar winner, Charlie Ross who is still looking wonderful despite being 48!

Well, it's a fantasy! I can indulge myself, can't I? But here's the real question, is this scenario as ridiculous as it sounds? The law has changed in support of gay rights in just about every conceivable way. Coming out isn't quite the trauma it used to be. Most self-respecting parents are now planning three children, one of each! I know some friends who are going to be gutted if one of their children isn't gay. Now I'm not kidding myself that we don't still live in a world with homophobia, and life for gay and lesbians isn't without its challenges. But things are definitely on the up. Yet the world of film stars, major celebrities and sporting heroes seems to be reluctant to embrace this brave new world.

There have been rumours about many movie stars for years. And Hollywood's history is littered with many posthumous collapses of the closet. As well as Rock Hudson, Montgomery Clift is now openly acknowledged as being a lifter of the occasional shirt, and it's pretty much agreed that the iconic James Dean was at least bisexual. But it all seems a case of too little, too late.

Do our major film stars really have to wait until they're pushing up the daisies before they can come out of the celluloid closet?

The first argument is that audiences wouldn't take actors seriously as hulking, hetero heart-throbs if they knew they were baking quiche and alphabetising their Barbra Streisand collection of an evening. Apparently we don't have the savvy to believe that Daniel Craig could possibly woo the endless ladies he does as James Bond if his sexuality was in any way questioned. Because that's the point, being a gay man is still perceived as being weak, timid and soft. Gay men can't be tough and lesbians can't be feminine. There's no way a gay actor would be believed if he were saving the world from terrorists, or Spider Man battling Venom or the Sandman. No, according to the movie executives we can't take that in. Our little brains wouldn't be able to process that information. Thing is, last time I checked, Tobey Maguire can't actually climb walls and spin webs, and I'm pretty sure Daniel Craig has never worked for MI6.

Here's the breaking news, they're ACTORS! And pretty good ones at that. The job is to make the audience suspend their disbelief and buy into the character on the screen. I sat in wonder throughout Casino Royale and one of the great things about it is the guy on the screen was James Bond, NOT actor Daniel Craig.

And that is a testament to Mr. Craig's skills and talent.

The public themselves aren't buying this myth either. They know that the world of actors has more than its fair share of gay men in it. I can still see the look on my parents faces when I told them I wanted to go to drama college, it was every parents fear that a son of theirs could want to go into "musical theatre".

It's no coincidence that Equity, the actors union, has a large and well supported LGBT committee. It's ridiculous to believe that every major movie star is a hettie. But the list of pretty young actors from Ryan Phillipe to Chris Evans (the Fantastic Four one, not the ginger!) are sold on their sexual appeal.

But that sexual appeal is sold to both girls and some boys. There is a misconception that girls who idolise these stars would lose their fantasy boyfriend if they knew he was gay. Well the key to that belief is the word "fantasy". Anyone can be a fantasy regardless of their sexuality. Apart from the real obsessives, who probably wouldn't believe it anyway, most fans know they're never actually going to get to shag Jesse Spencer. It can still be a fantasy! It's about education, that's all.

The world of sport is even further behind. Only Martina Navratilova and Greg Louganis fly that particular flag. The worst kept secret in British athletics about a certain retired hurdler has never been confirmed, despite being pretty nifty on Strictly Come Dancing. But the fear of being outed to the sporting community is haunted by the ghost of Justin Fashanu. The first professional footballer to come out, and whose life ended so tragically with his suicide amid accusations of sexual assault and abuse of trust. All underlining the belief that all gay men are predatory and promiscuous.

Again, there are rumours. Strangely, all the rumours tend to be about the cute ones. There are never rumours about the less attractive sports stars. I tend not to buy rumours about sports stars from the gay community. We can write those off as wishful thinking. Despite how many people tell you that "my best friend's mate's second cousin DEFINITELY gave Joe Cole a blow job in a sauna." It's the classic urban myth. And why not, it's all about titillation. But certainly in the world of football, it's the same conceit that a gay man can't hack it in a man's game. That we're not tough enough.

During a Fringe run a few years back I was asked to play football for the venue against another venue in the festival. A technician asked me if I was okay to tackle people, "can you handle it?" I was asked. This despite having played the bloody game to a pretty high level for a few years. His comment was met with the indignation it deserved. It's the only time I've ever felt inclined to kick a team mate during a match!

But it has to be said. There are 134 professional football clubs in the United Kingdom, with an average playing staff of 18 in each. That's 1,206 professional footballers. Is anyone, anywhere really going to tell me that every single one is completely, 100% heterosexual? Of course not. That would be ridiculous. Yet how are they living their lives? It's a shame, for we sadly know the answer. They are living a lie, a double life and are undoubtedly very unhappy. But that is the profession they have chosen. And there are clearly sacrifices to be made. But it is again a case of the gay person conforming to a prejudiced society. Tragic.

But why would one expect them to admit those details of their private lives when a casual glance at the press during the recent affair involving former Chief Executive of BP, Lord Browne, who quite rightly stepped down after being found to have lied in court, but the thrust of the story was not one of perjury but of his abilities to do this job because he was gay. The language was again implying that all older gay men want to get their hands on young men and all young gay men want to take everyone for everything they can get. It's wasn't a story about sexuality, but about opportunism. Yet the word "gay" is plastered all over the story. Would the word straight have been applied in equal measure had Jeff Chevalier – Lord Browne's former lover – been Jennifer Chevalier? I rather doubt it. Then the story would have been about, well, what the story was about.

I did once read an interview with a gay film star, albeit an anonymous one... au naturel! The rule of thumb that he applied was, if a top film star does an interview and mentions his wife or girlfriend three times in the first 5 minutes, he's probably gay. So, as you all reach for your back issues of every celebrity magazine you've ever bought to apply that theory it's interesting to note that Oscar Wilde, surely the biggest celebrity of his day, paid the ultimate price for coming out. It's a shame that the modern pampered and over-indulged celebs don't hold themselves to as high a standard!

The Showbiz Closet – it's a Tight Squeeze in There!
ScotsGay Magazine, February 2009

The words "Wolfenden Report" have been touted around this year, given that its fifty years since Lord Wolfenden recommended that homosexuality be decriminalised. It seems almost bizarre now that it was ever so, and still it took ten further years to actually get round to it. Films and television have portrayed gay and lesbian characters to varying degrees over those fifty years, and naturally things have got a lot better. Haven't they?

In 1961 Dirk Bogarde exclaimed the line, "Because I wanted him!" in the film *Victim*, finally giving a voice to the many gay men who were victims of blackmail. In fact, the highest incidence of blackmail cases were amongst homosexuals. There is a quote from the film itself, "Some say the law against homosexuality should be called the Blackmailer's Charter." Damn, even the word "ho-mo-sex-u-al" sounds ancient these days, so yes things have moved on a lot, and yes, popular culture has loads to do with that. Ground-breaking as *Victim* was, it was dark, depressing and perpetuated a notion that gay is dirty, gay is perverse, gay is undesirable, gay is, well, not that gay!

In the time since then, gay characters and story-lines have certainly taken on a new life of their own. The gays have been villains like The Krays (factual yes, positive, erm, no), serial killers in *Silence of the Lambs* – and there have been loads more of those, suicidal angst ridden teenagers like Sal Mineo whose character Plato lusts after James Dean in *Rebel Without A Cause* – well who didn't? Deep dark depression in dramas like *Lost Language of Cranes*, or all of the above only with AIDS thrown in. The alternative to this was the camp court jester, the asexual mincing queen who was always "free" and willing to allow their lifestyle and sexuality to be the butt of any and all jokes around.

Soaps and comedies have always flirted with it. Maureen Lipman's best friends in the 70's comedy *Agony* were gay. They only ever hugged of course, and naturally, one died. Huge US soap *Dynasty* made a big step and introduced a major gay character. The pretty Steven Carrington had boyfriends, whom he only ever hugged of course and jumped in and out the closet more often than the Narnia children. He even got a knock on the head that turned him straight – NO SHIT! Seriously! The original actor Al Corley, and to his eternal credit, quit the show after this in protest, even though he himself is straight. Only to be replaced by Jack Coleman, now famous from *Heroes*, but Hollywood had shown its true colours about this being an area they were very nervous about.

Eastenders introduced Micheal Cashman's Colin. He had little cuddly Barry as his boyfriend. They had coming-out storylines, HIV scare storylines, family ignoring you because you're gay storylines. In fact every gay stereotyped storyline you can imagine, because, you see, the story of the lives of gay people is only really about them being gay. They don't win the lottery, or have a drink problem (unless it's as a result of their inability to accept their, yep you guessed it, homosexuality!). And of course, they only ever hugged.

But it was a step, quite a big one. And, well, at least we should be thankful they hugged. If sitcoms of the time were anything to go by, gay men never had any kind of contact at all. But they did give us all a laugh. *Are You Being Served?* and *It Ain't Half Hot Mum* had two characters that were so dear to our hearts. The ultimate gay friend: funny, warm, charming and utterly asexual. Can you really imagine John Inman's Mr Humphreys getting it on with Mervyn Hayes Gloria? Now there's a sentence I never thought I'd write! In the 70's, the only role gays on TV seemed to fill was the court jester. Easy to spot, easy to pigeon-hole and easy to avoid all those nasty thoughts of two men together. Eugh! Sends a shiver down your spine, doesn't it?

Films like *Another Country* and *Maurice* dallied with gay leads the Merchant Ivory way, all floppy hair and posh accents. *The Krays* had no floppy hair and the accents were far from Eton-esque, and unlike the posh boy stories, all the lads went to see it. I clearly remember sitting in the cinema watching swords incising hands on snooker tables, mouths torn apart by hatchets and ritual killings in the East End's ganglands. The audience lapped it up, unflinchingly taking in all the violence. The only groan coming when Gary Kemp's Reggie kissed his male lover. What a fluffy and warm society we live in. I was very proud to be human that day.

Baby steps they may have been, but steps forward nonetheless. Things have moved on, and it is now apparently the law to crowbar a gay character into any available storyline. *Shameless* displays of snogging and sex have introduced a whole new world to straight viewers who could previously only imagine what two men or two women did in their intimate moments. For the average straight guy, the former with revulsion and the latter with the ultimate fantasy.

Eleven years ago, a little British film hit the big screen. It was a love story between two teenagers on a London housing estate. Despite family problems, school bullying and a distinct lack of enough peppermint foot lotion, their love blossoms. The audience are treated to a fairytale ending, as the two lovers embrace each other in the setting sun, dancing to a classic summer tune. Sounds like a fairly average story yes? Only the teenagers were boys. The film was *Beautiful Thing*. And it marked a turning point in the way gay characters were portrayed on the screen.

But back in 1996, Jonathan Harvey's little gem brought Ste and his neighbour Jamie together on a south London housing estate. It was fresh and new, neither was a posh public schoolboy from an E.M Forster novel. Nobody was suicidal, and the HIV virus was nowhere to be seen. It didn't depict a perfect coming out story, there was angst and anger, pressure and pain, but there was humour and wit and a sweet air of positivity that had never been seen on screen in a gay context. The boys snogged, clearly had sex and were even allowed something that gay storylines had rarely, oh lets be honest, pretty much never been allowed. Romance. Harvey Fierstein's Torch Song Trilogy aside, gay stories could never aspire to the *Breakfast At Tiffany's* moments, of falling in love on a rain-swept New York sidewalk. Because the popular myth was that gay people don't fall in love. They have sex. Nothing but sex. And lots of it. Mostly sordid and mostly casual. *Beautiful Thing* began the path that sorted that out. And gosh, how things have moved on.

Things were about to change. And a writer from Swansea with a passion for *Doctor Who* had plans afoot to take over the universe. But not before he showed the world the joys of a little street in Manchester. *Queer as Folk* was all about the homos. All the leads were gay. And the show depicted their entire world. Shirts were lifted, big time! We saw everything from foreplay to threesomes. Indeed, Russell T Davies probably introduced a whole new range of sexual practices to a mainstream audience. Without him, a later *Little Britain* gag would have died on its back-side. This was bold and brash television. And confirmed that audiences could cope with hard hitting scenes involving gay sex. Despite the lovely people at Beck's beer withdrawing their on-screen sponsorship of the show after one episode, *Queer As Folk* became a huge hit. And not just among gay viewers. The stories of Stuart, Vince and Nathan brought in millions and has even spawned an American equivalent which has recently completed its 5th and final season. So, in this fashion, the world of film and television went for it. Gay characters have been popping up everywhere. Lesbians in *Eastenders*. Gay nurses in *Holby City*. Even our beloved Corrie couldn't stay in the cold for long. And here is where the cracks started to show. A gay kiss in Holby brought the usual complaints. Probably the same number of complaints *Gardener's*

World gets when it misnames a plant – and probably from the same people – but of course the press jump on this at every opportunity. Pretty soon, those two characters were out the door. One was even killed, just to make sure.

They were brave. Very brave. Despite the fact that big build up of Bruno Langley's Todd, towards a stolen kiss with aspiring Tory MP Adam Rickett turned out to be no more than a New Year's kiss with your auntie. But oh, how they built it up. But to finally give every gay teenager a proper bona fide poster boy in the shape of the very pretty Mr Langley, was a brave move. And a positive one. *Coronation Street* had done it. Well of course it would. The best soap, created and written by gay men. We always knew that Corrie would come to the rescue and wouldn't let us down.

This wasn't Martine McCutcheon's fat ugly brother, or those infinitely dull blokes from *Brookside* who made the word gay seem bitterly ironic. This was real out and out, sexy, sassy Todd. He stood up to the Weatherfield dissenters, and brought a real sexy poof to the Street. But before you know it, he's gone and replaced by the ever popular camp character, two DNA strands away from John Inman and even with a job in the factory on a sewing machine. The sex was gone. The court jester was back. Coincidence? Or panic? Somewhere in the Corrie writing machine, they realised that Todd was cute, he'd go to Canal Street, he'd meet a boyfriend, he would have sex. Easy to show the occasional one-off "morning after" scene in the middle of a hard-hitting storyline. But to sustain it?

No, the Corrie fans would never put up with that. Well, of course they would. But it was too much of a risk. I know that Sean, played by Anthony Cotton, is an extremely popular character. But hasn't that always been the case? It's the safe gay route. Those characters are not really seen as overtly sexual. And they aren't pin-ups. Is that what a 14 year old gay girl or boy wants to see? Is he their fantasy? Because their straight counterparts get plenty of fantasies. It was starting to appear that the work of *Beautiful Thing* and *Queer As Folk* was for nothing.

But still the gay characters kept coming. Sonia was a part-time lesbian in *Eastenders*. Naturally she jumped back in the closet, they even made her girlfriend black just so that they could tick another box. And of course the black lesbian was the nasty piece of work that turned Sonia away from hetero perfection with Martin into the seedy world of lesbo love. The gay character was the villain again. And managing to underline the post-Clause 28 society that young people could indeed be corrupted and turned by nasty homosexuals. But at least they were there, and visible. Better than nothing, I suppose.

And on the big screen, *The Birdcage* was brilliant. But they only ever hugged. Bridget Jones naturally has a gay friend, even made the word poof innocent and funny again. But he doesn't have sex, does he? In fact, all of mainstream film and television were falling over themselves to bring gay characters to the screen. As long as they don't touch each other, in fact, here's the writing brief. Make sure they stand at least 10 feet away from each other, and throw some awkward furniture between them for good measure, just so they don't accidentally bump into each other.

With *Brokeback Mountain,* the phrase camping took on a whole new meaning, and gave us the easiest porn movie title in history (I'll let you work that out for yourselves!). No holds were barred, and no punches were pulled. Messrs Ledger and Gyllenhaal went for it. It wasn't the cheeriest viewing, but it did introduce the world to the notion that being gay doesn't mean dancing frantically to high-energy music, loving Kylie and having a secret quiche recipe. It told us (what of course WE already know) that gay men and women are everywhere. Everyone has met a gay person, you just didn't know it at the time. *Brokeback* isn't a great film, but it's an important one. Despite Heath Ledger's obvious discomfort with the kissing scenes - he even refers to his clear disgust at the notion in various promotional interviews he gave for the film. Hopefully

Hollywood will recognise that its foundations didn't come crumbling down because it dared to put gay subject matter in a mainstream movie and continue on that particular brick road, whatever colour it may be.

Back in the UK there is *Shameless*. Brilliant. Much revered, with plaudits coming from viewers and critics alike. Multi-award-winning, brilliantly written and realised. And a new kind of gay character. Of course not the cutest one in the family, but still Ian Gallagher is hard as nails with a slightly sensitive side. He has sex and has no problems with being gay, despite living on the Chatsworth Estate, which does at times seem like hell on Earth. But, here's the rub. In that there isn't really any. Rubbing that is. Every character has scenes of wild, romping sex. Ian's character has the occasional hand holding, odd snog and maybe the ripping off each other's clothes before cutting to the post-coital moment when one or the other is already downstairs making a cup of tea.

Now, the character is out there, and will be a positive connection to a lot of gay teenagers. But here's the thing. In an episode in the most recent series, Ian encounters a young girl with whom he strikes up a friendship, and ultimately an attraction. No objection there, interesting story and worth investigating. Lots of people both gay and straight often experiment with the alternatives. But in this episode, there were scenes of real passion, slow, soft and tactile. The sex scenes were tender and frequent, almost to the point where Ian is showing true affection for this girl. In fact, and I timed this – I know sad isn't it? - there was more on-screen time of Ian Gallagher being tactile with this girl in one episode than there were of him with any other guy in all episodes and seasons prior to that. Of course the next week he had a fling with the gangster next door, whom Ian totally used for sex, and despite the other guy being prepared to come out to his nutter family to declare his love for Ian, the young Mr Gallagher totally dumped on him and ruined his life. Because that's how gay men behave. Casual and emotionless sex lives, with no regard for the consequences.

But we do not despair. At 6.30 every evening, a little Channel 4 show called *Hollyoaks* is doing us all proud. I've not been the biggest fan of the cute girls and boys of Chester who really should spend most of their spare time on acting lessons. But the story of John-Paul's coming out has been dealt with sensitively, dramatically and very sexily. No awkward furniture between him and Craig. No, while you're biting into your crispy pancake and chips, the boys from Hollyoaks are getting it on big time. Well done Channel 4! Until, of course it all went Pete Tong and Craig got shipped off to Ireland. It will doubtless be a matter of time before John-Paul is left paralysed and impotent in a cruising accident outside a public toilet.

Bizarrely the BBC's own darling, *Doctor Who,* has been stealthily doing its bit for the cause. The Doctor's totally non-judgemental and unprejudiced view of species of all shapes, sizes and orientations, as well as pansexual Captain Jack Harkness, is a breath of Saturday evening fresh air. Spreading the word to a younger generation that it's ok to be gay. Even the Doctor says so.

So in this 40th anniversary of the decriminalisation of homosexuality in England, the gay community enjoys freedoms of equality that campaigners could only have dreamt when the Wolfenden Report was published. But on-screen, despite all the great work that has been done, there is a little bit to go. There is still a sense of nervousness and tension among producers of film and television when the subject is dealt with.

But the answer is simple. I long for the day when the new prime-time detective, now that Morse and Jane Tennyson have gone, comes home from a hard day hunting down a serial killer, to be greeted by his or her same sex partner. No major storyline, no gay scandal, just the way it is. A sub-text. A fact. Not an intrinsic part of the plot, just an aspect to the character. Or perhaps a storyline in a soap where the narrative for the gay character isn't about them being gay. The drama need not come from their sexuality. I don't think it is far away, as long as the likes of Jonathan Harvey or Russell T Davies are about, the future could be in safe gay hands.

Since writing this article, some of the TV shows have made some progressive moves. Eastenders *has introduced a ground-breaking storyline of the relationship between Londoner and an Asian Muslim. This has been handled well, and with integrity, and as we go to press the story seems to be putting them into a fairly positive relationship.*

In Emmerdale, *an excellent storyline involving bad lad Aaron Livesy became a touching and heart-rendering coming-out tale, written very well and played beautifully by young actor Danny Miller. The character has been thrown very quickly into a relationship which is a little unlikely for a young lad. Not impossible, but just seemed to move a little quickly. You see, what they can't really portray at 7pm on a weeknight, is the promiscuous life of a young gay man. So giving him a boyfriend is somewhat easier. Of course, again I have no idea how this will pan out and I may be completely contradicted, and you know what? I bloody hope so! But good on both those shows for dealing with homosexuality in a way that is sympathetic, yet dramatic and engaging.*

New Ball Please?
ScotsGay Magazine, August 2006

The Gay Games has just finished in Chicago. The event has grown over the last decade and is hugely popular. So much so that Richard Daley, Mayor of Chicago, thinks that hosting the Gay Games will benefit his city's bid to host the Olympics in 2016.

Yet the strange thing is that sport is still a no-go area for many gay people. Bad memories of PE lessons, playing with the rough lads at school and being forced to shower with everyone else, often suffering the ritual humiliation that children can inflict on each other. Experiences like that can be associated with sport, and particularly team sports like rugby and football, and can put gay men off popping down to the local sports centre for a game of tennis, or joining the local football club. However the paradox is that many gay women enjoy and participate in all kinds of sport. The most famous and obvious example is Martina Navratilova, but aside from the occasional ice dancer, gay men don't have an out professional sportsman who may help to increase the profile of sports participation among gay men.

Things are getting better. For those lucky enough to live in London or Manchester there are many opportunities to play football, rugby, tennis, even volleyball with other gay people. But this hasn't quite extended north of the border. I once put a notice up in Glasgow's LGBT centre to try and start a gay 5-a-sides night. I got 3 replies, one was from a straight mate of mine trying to support me! So why do Scots gay men have such an aversion to sport?

It's not as if gay men don't like fitness or physical activity. I'm sure many a punter in the Polo Lounge or Bennett's of a

Saturday evening is carrying a gym membership card in their wallet. Spending a few hours at the gym two or three times a week is an extremely popular pastime for gay men. Whether it's keeping trim, attempting to stave off the effects of getting older (yeah I know, tragic innit?), or searching for those Timberlake-esque abs that will have any guy in Delmonica's falling at your feet, the gym is not a place where gay men are scared to go. But the arena of sports participation is still a no-go area. I have always stayed fit to play sport. As a keen footballer, I have always played. Mostly for, and I hate to use the phrase, straight teams, and I certainly was the only gay in the village! But on only one occasion did anyone in the club know that I was gay, and even then it wasn't common knowledge. Is this the last acceptable form of prejudice?

There is the common misconception in society that sport is too rough for gay men. That they are too effete and basically ain't MAN enough. We all know this isn't the case. Some of the toughest people I know are gay, we have to be! It is a little hard to believe that of the 100 odd professional football clubs in the UK, with a squad of approximately 22 players at each, there are no gay footballers. Now yeah, we've all heard rumours. Funny how the rumours are always about the best-looking and cutest players. I never heard a rumour that former Rangers player Davie Dodds might be gay (to put you in the picture, his nickname was Elephant Man!), but it is reasonable to suggest that at least a small percentage is gay. Of course they are very closeted, and the fear of how they will be treated in the media, by the fans and by their fellow professionals. My background is in sport and as a fully qualified SFA coach, I was appointed under-18 coach to a professional Scottish club. Once someone at the club found out that I was gay, I was sacked. This happened 10 years ago. Maybe these days I may have been more tempted to take that further, but it was quite acceptable to fire me from a job I was eminently qualified to do, and had been very successful at. Because among certain circles being gay means that you can't keep your hands to yourself. Or that I would use my position to take advantage of the situation. This is no more ridiculous than suggesting a male PE teacher shouldn't teach Sixth Form girls for fear of the same kind of abuse. So if football still has this prejudice, then it is little wonder that any professional players don't come out or keep their feelings under wraps. The worst part of my experience was that I was told of my sacking by a club volunteer. The manager just wasn't man enough to look me in the eye and do it! But there is hope.

Ian Roberts is a professional Rugby League player from Australia. He came out publicly in 1994 and said that the reaction he got was generally positive. In some sense it would depend on the kind of player that did it. If a six foot solid defender who takes no prisoners on the pitch came out, he may find it a little easier than a wispy winger. The tragic tale of Justin Fashanu – to this day the only British professional sportsman to come out – may be enough to put off any other professional sportsman from coming out. There are British sportsmen, a famous athlete for example, who are gay but have never openly talked about it or stated it. Still wrapping themselves in ambiguity. There are those who would argue that why should they? They are doing a job and their sexuality has little to do with that. This is a good point, but the influence that an out gay sportsman could have on young gay men and women who like sport would be tremendous.

The situation will improve if gay people don't see sport as a purely heterosexual pastime, and that if you want to play, then take the opportunity. Find a club, or try to organise something amongst gay men. You don't have to be any good, it IS about the taking part. A bit of competition is healthy and playing sports is a great way to feel fit. There are already some clubs, a gay badminton group runs at Scotstoun Leisure Centre for example. And if you want to play sports, start a club yourself! So let's get in there, and take on the last thing that heterosexual society thinks it still has an exclusive hold on!

Again, as this article was written in 2006 it needs a little updating. In 2009, Welsh international rugby player Gareth Thomas came out, with a very sympathetic and positive outlook on his experience. This despite there also being an ex-wife involved. Many cities up and down the country now have gay football teams, even my home town of Glasgow has a team called Saltire Thistle, and Edinburgh's Hotscots F.C. have been operating for a few years now. I won't go any further on that now, but it's refreshing and good to note that things are moving on with regards to this area.

The Excess Factor
ScotsGay Magazine, September 2007

As another round of The X Factor is upon us, the endless weeks of car crash television, inflated egos, dashed hopes and dodgy telephone voting will grip the nation until Christmas. Quite cleverly, whipping the nation up into a frenzy over the hunt for the next Glen Medieros also ties in nicely with the festive panic where the true meaning of Christmas has been lost, so too has the true meaning of talent.

Talent shows have been around for as long as entertainment itself. A chance to show what you can, or in many cases, truly can't do, but, "go on, it'll be a laugh!"

In the 70's, Hughie Green brought opportunity knocking on our door and the faces on the other channel might have been new, but the acts certainly weren't. And occasionally, just occasionally, a star is discovered. Without talent shows we would have had to live without the urbane cutting wit of Jim Davidson. That would have been a national disaster, wouldn't it?

The talent show was always a bit of fun. The contestants were rarely far away from the Central Pier in Blackpool. No-one really took them seriously, and nobody ever expected a true star to emerge. The hunt for the next Lennon and McCartney or an emerging Monty Python crew never led to anything more than third rate acts who followed trends rather than set them. The ground of entertainment was never broken by a talent show winner. But that was fine. We sent our postcards to dear old Hughie at Teddington Lock and made a household name of

Les Dennis. Yes, really! No-one, but no-one could have seen the sinister side to all of this. Evil was at work.

The emergence of judges, "experts" if you will, came along and told the nation what it liked to be entertained by. Panellists who everyone loves to hate. At the forefront of this was Nina Myskow. Bolshy, brassy, rude, smug: qualities that the titular Miss Myskow would call honesty. She battered and bruised the egos of all in her wake, and started a very curious trend. She made the talent show about the judges and not the talent.

New Faces has regenerated Time Lord style into The X Factor. And the judges are the stars of the show. Uber-successful millionaires who gained fortune through staying in the wings and nudging the talent out there on the stage. At some point however, they must have realised that fortune really means nothing without fame. "But how can we achieve this fame of which you speak?" pleads the beige Louis Walsh. The talent of spotting talent isn't exactly a spectator sport. Go to see someone, they are either brilliant, good, average, seen it all before or mince. The true search for talent is going on all the time, in basement clubs and seedy music venues all over the country. The end product is what we want. The CD on the shelf or the download from an online music store. Aha, but there is mileage to be had out of replacing the polite knockback with out and out vitriol. Create a character. Time to give the talent show a villain of the piece.

It came in the form of "Nasty" Nigel Lythgoe on Popstars. He was bolshy, brassy, rude and smug – oh sorry Nina, eh – honest. With consummate tough love, he told the aspiring popsters what they had to hear if they were to make it in a cut-throat business where there is never a comfort zone. Always on your toes because the next big thing is just around the corner. I mean, look at David Bowie, Prince, Sting, U2, they all lived in fear throughout their careers of being knocked off the perch by the winner of Opportunity Knocks. Didn't they? Oh, no hang on. They weren't middle-of-the-road, half-baked attention seekers wanting to gain popularity out of yet another cover version of Unchained Melody; they actually have talent! Wow what a feeling that must be. The truly talented wouldn't be seen within a country mile of these shows, for fear, quite rightly, that any chance of respect in the business, or self-respect for that matter would be squandered forever.

For this is the cry of the talent show contestant. "This is my dream. It's always been my dream. I'll do anything to get there" Well, eh, no you won't. Anyone who truly follows a dream does a touch more than turn up at the SECC and stand in a queue to sing a karaoke number. No matter how good you are, or even if you win the thing, those who truly seek success in showbusiness get themselves out there. Singing lessons, acting lessons, paying to cut demos, performing gigs on any stage that is available, rapping on doors, and after the knocks have floored you, standing right up, dusting yourself down and keeping going. This is the road to success for the truly talented. The average take the quick route. The easy option where if it all fails, there is a panel of judges to blame for their mis-guidedness and lack of self awareness. But, as I said, talent shows aren't about the talent anyway.

Enter centre stage, Mr Simon Cowell. He has taken Nina's bolshiness, brassiness, rudeness and smugness and cleverly mixed it with Nigel's bolshiness, brassiness, rudeness and eh, smugness. And has of course added one thing, plain old fashioned badness. With Walsh and Osbourne sitting on their hind legs at his feet waiting for a chocolate drop to be thrown in their general direction, all three lord it over all and sundry who appear at the, ahem, auditions. As one vulnerable, attention seeking, needy, desperate-to-be-loved contestant after another breezes in the door, the three witches of this modern tragedy dole out insults like confetti, and laugh as they drag themselves out of the room, shattered, deflated and, if its possible, feeling even worse about themselves than they did five minutes earlier.

But hang on a moment. Aren't they all willing victims? Placing themselves at the mercy of the panel, fully cognisant of their fate. Well, not necessarily so. As any teacher or educational psychologist will tell you, negative behaviour amongst children, and indeed many adults, is as much a need for attention as singing a song in the local karaoke. Often any attention will replace none whatsoever. And if we fool ourselves by thinking that those who become the berated victims of the X Factor panel had any degree of self awareness, confidence or self belief, well they probably wouldn't be there in the first place.

This is where the sinister edge comes in. It might be couched in harmless fun, laughing at the vulnerable and the weak. But when three mega successful millionaires sit behind a table and celebrate with vindictive glee the downfall of those less fortunate than themselves, I begin to feel rather uncomfortable. If the show truly was about the talent, then why show the car crash contestants at all? Frankly because the *schadenfreude* is almost too much for us to ignore in the self-obsessed celebrity culture in which we live.

And the ones who can carry a tune in a bucket progress for further torment and trauma, made to believe that a week in a villa in Spain will make up for it. Even those who get through the final and derivative and clichéd. None have an ounce of originality, and rarely have a natural flair for the stage. They are middle-of-the-road clones of every other middle-of-the-road entertainer. One may wonder how the "experts" fail to spot this. Well, as a wise man once said, mediocrity knows no higher than itself, only true talent recognises genius. But then, not everyone can be a John Lennon or Madonna; my music collection has many a guilty pleasure and I'm thankful for it. My life is truly better for hearing "Yes sir, I can boogie" by Baccara, a troupe who would not look out of place on the X Factor, we just shouldn't be sold the premise that this programme is going to find a musical genius. And I'm guessing the judges know this. For they desire the biggest piece of this pie. They know that, aside from the substantial fortune that either Cowell or Walsh (whichever signs up the artists the public will take to their hearts), they will gain the fame and notoriety they seek. A win-win situation for them, a short career tossed on the pile of obscurity alongside Gareth Gates, Michelle McManus, and ... erm... the guy who won X Factor two years ago and, let's be honest, Will Young. Mr Young does indeed have considerable talent, but despite collaborations with the good and the great, even a movie with Dame Judi Dench, the smell of talent show winner is never far behind him. It is hard to shake off that particular stigma. Each and every one has gained the celebrity status they wished for. But like immortality, celebrity without substance is a curse.

The concept of celebrity in the 21st century has as much to do with talent as George Bush has with humility. The panellists on the X Factor are quite simply bullies. And the most dangerous kind. They are bullies with a budget. And influence. They prey on the weak, extort them for gratification and toss them away without a second thought. The X Factor is no more than The Jeremy Kyle Show with a glitterball.

So, consider this. On a Monday morning, in the cold harsh reality of a school playground, or indeed the workplace, and the vulnerable, as they always have been are brought before the bullies to be tormented and teased, how can we justify to that bully that what they are doing is wrong? We have sat and laughed and giggled at the victims of bullying on a Saturday night with fish and chips on our laps, snuggled up with our loved ones, all in the name of entertainment. Are we able to convince the playground bully that bullying is wrong, unjustified, cruel and unusual.

Hughie Green would be ashamed.

Hail to the millions who watch Doctor Who, Robin Hood, Casualty or even the nature programmes on BBC2! They at least recognise that to truly search for talent, you need go no further than the remote in your hand.

The publication of this book was funded with pre-orders. The author and publisher extend their thanks to the following people:

Catherine Aitken
Sharron Alliston
Prakash Bakrania
Lesley Byrne
Pau Gros Calsina
George Cameron
Stuart Cartwright
Mike Cook
Martyn Craigs
Sean Donnellan
Paul Dunn
Belinda Gallacher
Kevin Green
Henry Greenwood
Daniel Humes
Julian Innes
Lone Kristensen
Iain MacFadyen
Tom Mackay
Lewis MacKenzie
David McCahill
Scott McGeoch

Barry D McGirr
Martin McHarrie
Isabella Morrison
Jacqueline Murphy
Donald Nelson
Bruce Nicol
Lindsay Peebles
Jamie Renwick
Stan Rodgers
Jacqueline Shaw
James Shields
James Sterling
Keith Temple
Graeme Thaw
Gary Thomas
Rhys Thompson
Lesley Waite
Kevin Welsh
Gordon White
Steven Williamson
Cary Woodward

Do you have a book to publish?

A brand new concept in publishing.

As an author, you get:

100% of the profits from your book
100% control
100 copies of your book delivered to your door

and lots more.

www.100publishing.com

Also from 100 Publishing

Unconventional
By Karen Louise Hayward

At the age of 27, Karen Louise Hayward was living a conventional life as a married mother of four children in rural Lincolnshire. Then a trip to see Colin Baker in pantomime reawakened her love for Doctor Who.

In 1997, she met Colin Baker for the first time. Eager to see him again, she began travelling to conventions and events up and down the country. By the end of the year, not only did Colin know her, but so did several other of the Doctor Who actors. What's more, she had met her future husband at a Doctor Who event!

For the next thirteen years, it became a regular occurrence for her to meet the stars, listen to their interviews and get their autographs. But she did so much more besides…

- Proposing to Colin Baker
- Becoming pen-pals with Anthony Ainley
- Playing charades with John Nathan-Turner
- Going on a horse-drawn canal boat trip with Katy Manning
- Building a K9 out of clay for John Leeson

And all the time proving that being unconventional is the best way to be.

Written in a chatty, fun and light-hearted style, Un-conventional should trigger fond memories for the regular convention goer. And for those that have never been to a Doctor Who event and wonder what all the fuss is about, this book will explain all!

www.100publishing.com

Also from www.hirstpublishing.com

Look Who's Talking
By Colin Baker

To many, Colin Baker is the sixth Doctor Who; to some, he is the villainous Paul Merroney in the classic BBC drama The Brothers. But to the residents of South Buckinghamshire he is a weekly voice of sanity in a world that seems intent on confounding him. Marking the 15th anniversary of his regular feature in the Bucks Free Press, this compilation includes over 100 of his most entertaining columns, from 1995 to 2009, complete with new linking material. With fierce intelligence and a wicked sense of humour, Colin tackles everything from the absurdities of political correctness to the joys of being an actor, slipping in vivid childhood memories, international adventures and current affairs in a relentless rollercoaster of reflections, gripes and anecdotes. Pulling no punches, taking no prisoners and sparing no detail, the ups and downs of Colin life are shared with panache, honesty and clarity, and they are every bit as entertaining and surreal as his trips in that famous police box... for a world that is bewildering, surprising and wondrous, one need look no further than modern Britain, and Colin Baker is here to help you make sense of it all, and to give you a good laugh along the way.

Also from www.hirstpublishing.com

Self Portrait
By Anneke Wills

This is a moving, witty and candid account of a fascinating life among the talents who defined the swinging sixties. Appearing in ground-breaking television from an early age, Anneke Wills was one of the busiest actresses of the 1960s – her role as Polly establishing a template for one of television's most iconic and prized roles – the glamorous Doctor Who girl. This is a beautifully written story of a unique childhood, life at the heart of swinging sixties London, and a turbulent marriage to a leading actor. Anneke's life revolved around the eccentrics, actors, film-makers, painters, designers, poets, satirists and drunks who were changing the world. She counted among her friends the leading lights of the time – from Peter Cook to Sammy Davis Jnr. Illustrated in full colour with previously unseen photographs and Anneke's own drawings and paintings, this is the story of a rich and colourful life, and the growth of a truly remarkable woman.

Also available:
Naked, by Anneke Wills
(volume 2 of her extraordinary autobiography)

Also from www.hirstpublishing.com

Flight Risks
By Douglas Schofield

Basel, Switzerland, February 2001 : Fifty-six years after the end of World War Two, Switzerland's bankers finally agree to release 21,000 dormant accounts left behind by Jews who died in the Holocaust. Claims from the victims' heirs pour in from across the world...

New York and Washington, September 2001 : The Twin Towers fall. The Pentagon burns. Western democracies scramble to meet a deadly new threat...

Victoria, Canada, October 2001: For legal secretary Grace Palliser, the post-911 media circus is just background noise. Grace is too busy with the unholy mess she calls her life. But when she stumbles on evidence of a vast international fraud, her life gets a whole lot messier. Framed for murder and desperately searching for the evidence that will clear her, Grace flees across the continent to New Orleans, then to the Florida Panhandle, and finally to a small island in the northwest Caribbean. Hot on her trail is a corrupt former cop with a simple assignment - to Kill Grace Palliser.